To my Charm...
Philippa;

BASS LINES

A LIFE IN JAZZ

Long may you continue
to enjoy Radiant Health,
Happiness, Good Company,
and the Best Things in Life!

Coleridge Goode.
5/9/04

Coleridge Goode
and
Roger Cotterrell

BASS LINES
A LIFE IN JAZZ

orthway
publications

Published by Northway Publications
39 Tytherton Road, London N19 4PZ, UK
www.northwaybooks.com

Cover design by Stewart Aplin, Aplin Clark, London EC1

Cover photos: Ray Ellington and Coleridge Goode c1948
(photo by S. L. Fry); Joe Harriott Quintet c1959 (Photography
33, London).

The publishers acknowledge with thanks the kind permission
of copyright holders to reprint the photographs used in this
book. Permissions have been sought in all cases where the
identity of copyright holders is known.

A CIP record for this book is available from the British Library.

ISBN 0 9537040-2-5

First published 2002

Printed and bound in Great Britain by Antony Rowe Ltd,
Chippenham, Wiltshire

Contents

introduction

Coleridge Goode needed persuading to tell his story, modest man that he is. But there are important reasons for telling it. As a highly regarded jazz instrumentalist his main career achievements have been of great artistic significance. And he is candid not only about the rewards and rich variety of life as a professional musician but also about serious social problems of the jazz world which he has seen at first hand. Not least, his account of his life in music gives a host of rich insights into neglected but important aspects of jazz history.

For example, he was a member, throughout its whole eight years existence, of the Joe Harriott Quintet – a musical unit which, as the years pass, becomes ever more legendary. Goode is the only person who can give a full account of this band and detail all the controversies that surrounded it. Many critics claim that this was the most historically significant and, at its peak in the early 1960s, the most original small group ever on the British jazz scene. Entirely alone and ahead of its time, it set new directions for jazz, developing a free form style distinct from but contemporaneous with Ornette Coleman's American developments. Goode's role as bassist was unique and crucial in Harriott's musical conception. But in the small world of British modern jazz, the quintet was praised and vilified with equal intensity among musicians and critics. The controversy has not been entirely resolved to this day and its high human costs are recalled in this book.

Yet the group's best albums have become classics. Before they were reissued on CD, the original LPs, 'rare as hen's teeth' to quote one retailer, fetched hundreds of pounds in auctions and were hunted by knowledgeable collectors on both sides of the Atlantic. Now this music is gradually acquiring the broader transatlantic recognition that is its due and in the 1990s, the leading Chicago contemporary jazz group of Ken Vandermark recorded an album of Harriott compositions associated with the quintet. The *Guinness Who's Who of Jazz* calls Harriott, 'one of the most inventive and original of jazz musicians... a major figure in the development of both a European Free Jazz tradition and a jazz-based fusion that incorporated elements of ethnic music.' Coleridge Goode, in a key role throughout, helped to make all these triumphs possible. In part then, this book is a celebration and a chance to set the record straight about major but still misunderstood jazz innovations.

Another reason for telling his story is that it is one of many possible accounts of the historical experience of black West Indian musicians in Britain and their contribution to the jazz scene. There is, of course, no single 'experience' to categorise. Goode's career is unique and has brought its own challenges and triumphs. Nevertheless, it has led him into contact over the decades with many other West Indian instrumentalists about whom he has interesting things to say. Since so little has been written about the contribution of West Indian musicians and black musicians more generally to the development of jazz in Europe, this book helps to document an unjustly neglected part of musical and cultural history. The personalities and talents of many unsung individuals who contributed, often with great distinctiveness, to music are recalled here with warmth and candour.

The best reason for this book, however, is simply Coleridge Goode himself – who he is and what he has done over the decades. For a long time he has been one of the most respected jazz bassists in Europe and the list of major international stars with whom he has worked and recorded is impressive, including Django Reinhardt, Stéphane Grappelli, Ray Nance and George Shearing, amongst many others.

He chooses words carefully and talks simply and honestly but his modesty does not disguise his pride in his craft and artistry and in the remarkable body of recorded music to which he has contributed. A man of dignity and integrity, he has managed to combine idealism about the infinite possibilities of music with realism about the darker sides of the jazz life. He has kept a clear sense of direction while often working in a social environment full of individuals with much less stable and sometimes seriously blighted lives. What is said in the following pages about Joe Harriott, Phil Seamen, Shake Keane, Lars Gullin, Lauderic Caton and many others suggests something of this environment, although the book is very much a celebration of everything that outstanding players such as these have given to jazz.

After growing up in a secure family environment in Jamaica, Coleridge made a similarly stable life for himself when he moved to Britain. Discipline and self-reliance are words he very often uses when he talks about the inheritance his childhood gave him. A longstanding friend of his told me: 'Coleridge is a rock. He was always the stable point we could rely on when all kinds of things were falling apart.'

He is a survivor, the man who lived to tell the tale: his own and, indirectly, that of some other notable musicians in so far as they have been a part of his world.

He was nineteen when he stepped off the boat in 1934 to begin a new life in Britain. At that time few made the one-way journey from the Caribbean to settle and he came initially as a student. Music was not planned as his career but it was certainly in his background. In Jamaica early in the twentieth century his father almost single-handedly set out to create a vibrant musical life in the church communities of Kingston. The concerts, competitions and festivals, Bach cantatas and oratorios and the whole life of choral classical music, with his father at its centre, left indelible imprints on the young Coleridge. But, with no possibilities for a career in classical music in Jamaica, he chose to study engineering. Then fate intervened. He heard a wealth of jazz on records and, giving up the violin on which he had played the classical repertoire of his youth, he mastered the double bass and launched himself on a jazz career.

In the following pages he recounts his early life in Jamaica and Glasgow and his career, starting with the lively musical life of wartime London clubs. A key figure in every band with which he has worked, he tells of life on the road with the Ray Ellington Quartet of 'Goon Show' fame, which achieved immense popular success combining the new modern jazz sounds of the late 1940s with zany humour. Later, with other bands, there were different experiences of selling 'bop for the people', trying to create adventurous jazz music in dance-halls and clubs in 1950s Britain while avoiding the twin curses of racism and drugs. Throughout the period he established himself at the very centre of the London modern jazz world.

In 1958 Goode joined the new band being formed by the brilliant bebop stylist Joe Harriott. But Harriott's early audiences had little idea what was in store as his musical development unfolded over the following decade. Goode provides an unforgettable portrait of the alto saxophonist, describing how his pathbreaking 'abstract music' came about and the triumphs and disappointments that went with it. Later, Harriott's searchings took him into other new territory, producing some of the earliest and still most successful fusions of jazz and Indian music. Again, Goode's bass played a key role, linking the jazz and Indian components of the music.

In more recent years he has found himself in many other musical contexts, usually at the cutting edge, among the innovators. He recorded serial music with David Mack and participated in the poetry and jazz movement that was a significant artistic development in Britain from the 1960s. He has been an important contributor to ambitious experiments with choral and religious settings for jazz. Perhaps the wheel came full circle in one sense with a distant echo of his father's choral work in Goode's participation in Michael Garrick's orchestral performances with choirs in church settings.

When he began to look back over his career as plans took shape to produce this narrative he wondered whether his life was really of sufficient interest to merit a book. 'I don't want to bore people,' he insisted. I had no doubts and took it on myself to convince him. In the following months, having agreed experimentally at my urging, to 'give it a try and see how the conversations go', we taped many hours of his reminiscences and talked over innumerable subjects. I wrote the narrative in continual consultation with him, using the taped conversations as the basic material for the text and combining his memories with my background research. Coleridge has checked the whole text and approved its final form. Talking at length with him and assembling the story has been, for me, a great privilege and hugely pleasurable experience.

This book, the outcome of our many meetings in front of teapot, cassette recorder and audio system, recounts Coleridge Goode's remarkable adventures in music and his well-fulfilled life from Jamaica to jazz.

ROGER COTTERRELL

1.

100 miles to Cuba

My music room is high above a London street. From here, you don't hear pedestrians on the tree-lined pavement below or, with the window closed, much traffic sound. In a corner by the window an old battered double bass rests on its stand. It's the bass I learned to play jazz on more than sixty years ago when I set out to become a professional musician and I still use it today. I've had it since I was in Glasgow as a student. It was nearly burnt by a blazing fire and it once fell off a tramcar. But it's a good instrument which has associated with a lot of wonderful musicians. Next to it are a high stool and footstool with metal folding struts, which I use when I play.

Behind is an audio system I made myself. Most of the parts are old but it sounds state of the art. Science and technology have always been important in my makeup. Years ago, my friend Lauderic Caton and I made our first television sets at a time when few people had TV. In 1946 I designed and built an electronic amplifier for my bass. No-one used amplifiers on basses then and what I did was very controversial but I like to be heard when I play. And as a musician I'm used to hearing the sound of the instruments loud all around me so I'm right in the centre of it. The audio system creates that sound in the room from my records and cassettes.

Above the audio system are piles of cassettes in boxes. Among them are tape copies of many records on which I've played with 'Joe Harriott', 'Ray Ellington Quartet', 'Michael Garrick', 'Shake Keane' and other names on the labels. Unfortunately some great groups I played with never made studio recordings so almost all the music is lost now. But there are a lot of boxes of Harriott and Garrick and dozens of tapes from the informal Sunday jazz sessions in north London where I have played regularly since the 1970s. I tape the sessions to hear what I've done recently and see how I can improve on it.

On a shelf under the window is a biography of Stéphane Grappelli who, with George Shearing, was part of my professional life for some years. And in the other corner of the room by the window is where Django Reinhardt sat cradling my one year old daughter on his knee and talking in his animated French to my wife Gertrude. He visited us when I recorded with him in 1946, when he and Stéphane were reunited in London after being separated for the whole period of the war.

I keep this room warm. In the winter months when my co-author and I started to have regular conversations to plan this book, he would always strip off his sweater when he arrived here and was hit by the semi-greenhouse atmosphere that I like, especially when it's cold outside. After all the years of living in London I still find the weather too cold. I was conditioned to warmer climes. I came to Britain in 1934, leaving the Jamaica sunshine and heat behind and finding British rain and fog and grey Glasgow tenement blocks instead during my student days. A few years later I came to London and settled here. So this flat and this room have been my place for well over half a century, though I've travelled with my music to many countries and seen a fair bit of the world.

The area has changed a great deal. When Gertrude and I moved here, the whole block had been shocked to its foundations by wartime bombing. There were huge cracks in the ceiling of this room, caused by the explosions. Part of the block had been demolished by a German bomb some months earlier. At that time I was only the second West Indian in the neighbourhood. All that changed after the Windrush, of course. A lot has changed over the years.

......

I was born a few months after the First World War started in Europe, but on a different continent, thousands of miles away. The area where I grew up, St. Andrew, is a small county on the south eastern side of the Caribbean island of Jamaica. To the north east of St. Andrew are the beautiful, spectacular Blue Mountains. English people have sometimes heard of them because of the excellent Blue Mountain coffee. I was born on November 29th 1914 at Hope, six miles out of Kingston, the capital, and six hundred feet above sea level. From there it was a steady down hill drive to Kingston on the coast.

Jamaica was a British colony then and my father had a job in the colonial agricultural service. He lived and worked at a farm school, Hope Farm, which the government set up to train young people to become efficient farmers. Half a mile away from the farm, along the Hope Road, was an important food market called Papine, a big centre for selling produce, not far from where the University of the West Indies is situated today. When I was a small boy trams ran along the Hope Road from Kingston, up the hill to the market at Papine. Women going up to Papine or down to Kingston market would load their vegetables into the back part of the tram and ride in the front. Later, when the trams were replaced by buses imported from England, there were always special compartments at the back and on top of the buses for the farm produce and the buses would crawl up to Papine with produce to be sold. But in the early days the transport system relied on trams powered from overhead electric wires. The trams would stop at the terminus at the market and then reverse and run back down the hill past Hope Farm towards the centre of Kingston.

The only neighbours we had were people who worked at the farm school and lived on the premises. It was a big complex with fruit trees that grew all around, stretching up towards the hills. The house I was born in was actually in the farm school grounds but later, when I was about ten, we moved to a nicer house at the entrance to Hope Gardens, the horticultural gardens where the school's head office was situated. Tram drivers used to stop at that point and punch a clock to indicate when they arrived.

The houses were wooden with bamboo furniture and polished wooden floors. The custom at the time was to split a dry coconut down the middle, put wax polish on the cut edge and rub it across the floorboards to make them shine. In our home the maids did this. When I was a boy there was no domestic electricity and we had pressurised paraffin lamps with mantles. Of course, in the hot climate the houses had plenty of window space and doorways to let the air circulate. When it cooled in the evening you could go and sit outside on the verandah in your rocking chair. That was the best time of day, when it was cool.

Roofs were often made of zinc because zinc gives really tough protection and when it rains in Jamaica it really rains. But the downside was that if there was a hurricane you would stand a good chance of having the zinc blown off the roof. That didn't happen to us, but it was not uncommon at all and there were plenty of hurricanes. A lot depended on where your house was situated. At a distance, facing our house, a mountain rose to about a thousand feet and gave protection against the winds. So the house was not as badly affected in the storms as it might have been.

With the zinc roofing, you would hear the rain beating on the roof very clearly when you were inside. Our house was just one storey – a bungalow, you would call it – and I used to love to hear the rain on the roof when I was in bed at night. It had a sort of lulling effect, helping to send me to sleep.

In the day I played in the garden and climbed the mango trees. Everyone had fruit trees in their yards. Mangoes, bananas, limes, paw-paws, all sorts of lovely fruits. And there were coconut palm trees. Jamaican vegetation is very lush. In our garden there was a jasmine bush at the side of the house. Of course, jasmine has a beautiful smell and in the cool of the evening the fragrance would waft around and drift inside the house through the doorways and windows.

My father had his own room which was his studio, full of books on music, literature and poetry. He had a large library there and also his organist's piano, fitted with two keyboards and pedals like a church organ. He used to practise on that. He was the organist and choirmaster at St. Michael's and All Angels Church in Victoria Avenue, Kingston during the time I was growing up and he held this position for more than fifty years. Music, especially choral and church music, was a big part of his life and, because of him, music became as big a part of mine, although he never really approved of the jazz I played when I became a professional musician. Music for him always meant classical and choral music, nothing else. I never heard any other kind of music as I grew up because we did not have a radio and classical music was all that was played at home.

George Davis Goode, my father, really was a self-made man. In 1903, when he was 21, he became an unpaid laboratory apprentice at the Government Laboratory at Hope. He learned about chemistry on the job. Then he won a scholarship to enter the Agricultural School and got a position in the new farm school when it was set up in 1910. He worked for the Agricultural Department until he retired and eventually he became Acting Assistant Director of Agriculture. But alongside all this he was busy with music.

At that time, nobody was doing anything like he did in the music line. Most music performed in Kingston was made by people accompanying silent films shown in a couple of theatres. Apart from that there wasn't really any professional musical activity. Music was limited to what local people produced at parties for their own amusement.

George Goode studied, listened to gramophone records and taught himself. Being organist at St. Michael's, he had to arrange all the music for the church choir. So he imported books and sheet music and studied how to go about it and produce what was required. When gramophones came in, we got the first wind-up model, a magnificent affair. But with those old record players the sound of the ordinary pick-up was not at all kind to the lower frequencies of the music on the records and the bass sounds didn't come through. So people would fit up what was called an exponential horn which accentuated the lower frequencies. With that big horn, most of the music on the record could be heard. It had to be fitted to the gramophone and from the fixing point to the end of the bell the horn increased in diameter like a huge dark flower that had opened out. I helped my father build it from the instructions that came in the kit. You had to make the hoops a certain size, fit them together, cover them with paper and then varnish the whole thing.

He taught himself to arrange music and create all kinds of

musical settings. The range and ambition of what he did was astonishing and eventually he put on oratorios and big choral performances, concerts and competitions. In 1909, the year before he became organist at St. Michael's, he married my mother, then Hilda Dawkins, who sang in the choir at Kingston Parish Church. She had a lovely soprano voice and supported him with all his musical enterprises. After a time they started the Kingston Glee Singers Society which put on annual concerts starting in 1912 and those concerts continued for 25 years. They would present mainly church music and when it came to doing bigger things, such as major works by Handel and Bach, the Glee Singers were joined by singers from the big Diocesan Festival Choir which my father organised.

All these activities became recognised as a major part of the musical life of Jamaica. In 1919 the *Jamaica Times* wrote:

> The Kingston Glee Singers form one of the satisfactory organisations in this Island devoted to those arts which help the mind and lend deeper degrees of beauty and interest to life. Life in a small community like ours tends persistently to fall into a routine, and to become merely a humdrum struggle for existence.... The Glee Singers... annual concert has gradually taken its place among the most distinctive and the most valued musical events of the year in the Island.

One story about how George Goode solved musical problems is told in a book about him which his secretary Ethel Marson wrote after his death. He read a publication called *Fugitive Notes on Certain Church Cantatas* by William Gillies Whittaker, a great Bach authority who edited Bach cantatas for Oxford University Press. In 1928, stimulated by the book, he decided to include in the Diocesan Festival Choir programme the cantata 'Sleepers, Wake'. As Ethel Marson puts it, 'he was not quite certain of the correct manner of interpreting some of the ornaments in the latter work, and with his usual careful attention to detail, he decided to seek Dr. Whittaker's advice.' So he wrote to the famous Bach expert far away on the other side of the ocean in England, explaining that, 'music is in a very backward state in this colony and I am trying to do my little bit...' Dr. Whittaker sent back detailed advice, said how pleased he was that Goode had found his books helpful, and wished him all the best. After that, they corresponded for years, Whittaker praising Goode's 'magnificent work' and 'fine influence' and telling him not to worry about critics who were 'always wrong' and from whom 'we all suffer'.

It must have been hard then to get enough good musicians to put together the orchestras to accompany the big choral works, but there was a military band in Jamaica and musicians were brought in from that. Later the military director of music incorporated some of the better players into an orchestra to play symphonic pieces. But my father originated all these big musical presentations. No-one else was trying to do anything like that at the time.

I got my name indirectly through the Glee Singers' activities. In 1912, the celebrated black British classical composer Samuel Coleridge-Taylor died. George Goode had the idea of organising a festival to honour his memory and it took place in September 1913. He put together a choir of a hundred voices and a thirty piece orchestra to perform two concerts of Coleridge-Taylor's music. The events made a huge impression at the time. There had not been any musical occasion to match this in Jamaica previously. I was born a year later and named Coleridge after Coleridge-Taylor. My other names are George, after my father, and Emerson, after the poet. My father loved poetry and Ralph Waldo Emerson was one of his favourites.

Music completely surrounded me when I was growing up. I must have always been drawn to it but it took a long while to discover my own way to approach it. My father tried to teach me the piano but for some reason I wasn't keen on that and it did nothing for me. Then I heard a cellist at one of my father's concerts. When I listened to this man, Leslie Thompson, playing a solo something just hit me. It was so lovely. After I got home, I found some bits of orange box wood and tried to make an instrument using ordinary twine for the strings. My father saw this and being a very wise man he gave me a violin on my next birthday, my eleventh or twelfth. So I was a late starter as a music student but after that I took to the violin straight away. Something drove me to do this. It was something I loved and I made very good progress.

Along the way I also had lessons on the oboe. I had heard the great English oboist Leon Goossens on records and that influenced me to take up the instrument. The oboe is still in a cupboard here somewhere but it is not one of the top makes and the fingering system is antiquated. Anyway, it didn't really work out for me. You have to have the right embouchure for that particular instrument and I could never maintain it for long.

The violin was my passion. In Kingston they started to have an annual musical competition to find the best pupils. There were a couple of really good violin teachers in the town and I was very lucky. I had the best, Doris Livingstone. She had flaming red hair and was a lovely person. I was very fond indeed of Miss Livingstone and that helped very much in learning the violin because I *always* wanted to go to lessons at her house! I studied with her for the examinations of the Royal Schools of Music – someone would be sent out from England each year to examine the pupils. I passed all the examinations year by year and eventually became a Licentiate of the Royal Schools of Music in about 1932.

At school, music and sport were what I liked best. After Montessori school, when I was nine or ten I started going to Calabar High School, one of the big secondary schools in

Kingston. I travelled by tram but when I was about thirteen I got a bicycle and cycled the six miles from Hope
Gardens. Later the bike was replaced by a motorcycle. I was
a day scholar like all the other children from the Kingston
area. But there were boarders too whose families lived in
other parts of the island, some from right over in Montego
Bay on the north coast. Every morning, school began with
chapel. The headmaster's son played the organ and I would
have a seat on the front bench in the chapel and play my
violin, accompanying the psalms and hymns. As for sport,
we played football and cricket which I've always loved.

The school produced many sportsmen, some quite
famous. One was Arthur Wint who became the Olympic
400 metres champion the year the games were held in
London. A statue was erected in his memory in Sabina Park
in Kingston. That was where the schools competed with
each other in the big annual sports day events. But Calabar
didn't really produce musicians, as I remember, apart from
me. Many Jamaican musicians who later became well
known in jazz came from a different school in Kingston
called the Alpha School, which catered especially for
orphans, children from poor families and children with disabilities. Joe Harriott, whom I'll have much to say about
later, was one of its products.

Of course, it was not just music and sport at school. We
covered all the subjects. History then – in the 1920s and
early 1930s – was all about the British Empire and there was
no Jamaican history taught at all. Some of the teachers were
black, some white. Several had come from England. The
science teacher, for example, was a Yorkshireman, Mr.
Wolstenholme. The school was mainly Baptist-run and the
headmaster and second master were Baptist ministers. And
there were certainly memorable people, such as Philip
Sherlock, who later became Vice-Chancellor of the
University of the West Indies. He was a great story-teller

for children. He used to tell us about the exploits of his uncle. 'Uncle' didn't really exist but Mr. Sherlock told us about his amazing adventures and we would sit wide-eyed.

One story was about 'Uncle' being out in the forest when suddenly he came upon a lion. 'What can I do?' he asked himself, terrified. When the lion attacked, opening his jaws to bite, 'Uncle' shoved his hand, quick as a flash, into the lion's mouth and right through his stomach and grabbed his tail and *pulled him right inside out!* And so he triumphed over the lion. What a feat! Mr. Sherlock was a wonderful teacher and a lovely person.

Life was filled with school, violin practice and sport. I would get up early and practise my violin before going to school and I would often come home late because of staying on for sports after lessons ended. Calabar was one of the best schools for sport in the country. I'm grateful now for all that sports activity because it made me strong. When I got home I would relax for a little while, then get on with homework and then maybe do some more practice on my violin. It was a strict upbringing with a lot of discipline.

With all that happening, I didn't see a great deal of my father in those years. He taught me all the rudiments I needed for my music examinations but, of course, he was always very busy too. He was a well-studied man and not at all ebullient – you could say he was reserved, but studiously reserved. And one thing I learned from him was how to be self-reliant. His example in that influenced me all my life.

My mother, Hilda Goode, was a lovely person. She used to lead the sopranos in both the church and the big concert choir. She had many friends and was one of eight or nine children, so there were a lot of aunties around. She was also a great cook and so I and my two sisters, Ruth and Helena, were very well looked after. She made all her own bread and

cakes and would make wedding cakes for friends. I used to
help with the icing. She liked to have tea parties and was
very proud of her special bone china tea set as they were
not easy to come by at that time in Jamaica.

St. Andrew changed a lot over the years I lived there. The
tramcars gave way to buses on the Hope Road and gradually the traffic increased around Kingston. But, of course, it
was nothing like the London traffic. Most cars were
American since Jamaica was so much closer geographically
to the United States than to Britain and the American cars
were cheaper to buy. I remember when one of the teachers
at the farm school bought a brand new English bullnose
Morris. He drove it, with its gleaming brass front and radi-
ator-top, up the drive to Hope Farm. What a sight! It was a
convertible with a canvas roof, and had lovely leather. The
smell of it! It was quite something, a very elegant thing in
those days and very unusual. This man used to go to
England every so often for holidays and he brought this
beauty back from one of his trips.

My father's car was an old Ford, a tin lizzy, one of those
three-pedal things in which you had to change gear with
your feet. He didn't travel much beyond the Kingston area
in it. But once in a while he would have to visit the extension of the agricultural school about fifty miles away in
Mandeville in the western part of the island. And on a couple of occasions I went with him high up into the Blue
Mountains to Cinchona. That was a beautiful, quiet spot to
relax and enjoy the scenery. The area had been planted with
Assam tea bushes and cinchona trees from which they produced quinine, then used for treating malaria. It was a commercial enterprise but apparently it didn't do well and eventually, in the late 1960s, it was turned into Government-run
public gardens. I don't know whether there was a link to
the Agricultural Department at the time we went there but

in any case, my father didn't take any of the employees from the Farm School.

We would travel part of the way by car until the mountain tracks became too difficult. Then we'd leave the car and get on donkeys to go up to this wonderful place, high up in the mountains where the air was clear and fresh.

One of the donkeys would be loaded with saddle bags with all the clothing and provisions. The animals were so sure-footed and you had to marvel at the way they climbed on that rough terrain. Up in the mountains it was very cool. There were pine trees and at Christmas time you might find strawberries. On a good clear day, because of the high elevation, you could look straight across the Caribbean and see Cuba in the distance about a hundred miles away. The temperature was in the low 50s (10 to 12 degrees Celsius), as I remember, and that to us was really cold. In the morning there would sometimes be just a little bit of frost on the vegetation.

All the time I lived in Jamaica I was aware that there was a difference between the races. You couldn't avoid that. In the first place, since the territory was a colony, the English always had the best of whatever jobs there were. There was always some English person in charge and it was the same in the Agricultural Department where my father worked. There was a white Director with overall responsibility and he lived in the exclusive lower part of the garden with his several English bulldogs. They were frightening and no-one would go there. My father was responsible directly to this Director. He would go away for three months holiday and my father would have to run the operation while the Director was away. Of course, he was fully capable of it and recognised as very able. He won medals for his civil service work: the King George V Silver Jubilee Medal in 1935, the King George VI Coronation Medal in 1936 and the

Insignia of the Imperial Service Order in the King's birthday Honours in 1942.

I didn't feel race prejudice affected me directly. I was always in the best of whatever was going on but there were certainly colour differences. The lighter-skinned mulattos were considered above the very dark people in this racial estimation. It was subtle but it was there. But in the musical world that existed, the world my father and mother were in the centre of, there was a mixture of all sorts of people. Race had no bearing at all on us and we mixed with the English. My violin teacher was English and we pupils, black and white, all went to school together and were mixed there. We learned not to discriminate like that. For my family, things were not bad. We were middle class and comfortably off. But elsewhere there was terrible poverty in Jamaica.

Eventually, when I was about seventeen, I had to begin to think seriously about what I might do for a career. In my earlier years I hadn't contemplated doing anything other than playing music. It was only later when I needed to consider how to earn a living that other thoughts came to mind. After all, even my father, with his great love of music and his talent for it, did not make a living from it.

I had an aptitude for mechanics and technology. Sam Kitchin, one of my father's closest friends, had a Douglas motorcycle with big cow-horn handlebars and eventually he let me try riding it. That really turned me on to motorbikes. Then one of my school friends, Guilfoyle, whose father was very wealthy, got himself a Douglas, a more modern model with normal handlebars. I decided to get an old second-hand BSA. So there were two of us who rode motorcycles to school. I used it for a couple of years and would lovingly take the machine apart, paint the frame and clean the points. So I learned about mechanics that way. The bike didn't have electric lights but carbide lighting. Water dripped down and made a gas which had to be lit in a burner at the front that threw the light out in a beam.

It was clear that Jamaica was going to need electrical engineers. Before electric light came to St. Andrew there was only gas and paraffin lighting. It took some time for electric lighting to become widespread and there was no road lighting at all before the electricity came so people did not travel much at night. Although the trams were electrically powered, the extension of electricity throughout Jamaica still had a a long way to go. Electrical engineering was like computer science is now, the new practical science to get into if you were ambitious.

In 1932 it was decided that I should go to a place called Cornwall College, in Montego Bay at the other end of the island, to study sciences further for a year in preparation for travelling to Britain to do a degree in electrical engineering at university.

Glasgow was chosen as the university for me to go to because it was famous for its engineering faculty and the town was famous for engineering. Also my father had a good connection there because his correspondence friend, Dr. Whittaker the Bach expert, had become the professor of music at Glasgow University.

It is hard to say whether engineering was a second best for me. I never lost any interest in music. I had an inate love of it. And what would actually happen when I reached Britain was always left in the air as far as I was concerned. If I obtained a university degree the option was open to me to do whatever I liked with it. I always felt that spending one's life producing or being involved in music was the way to go. But when I set off for Britain I could not see how to make a musical career so the plan was to get the best qualifications I could in electrical engineering and then come back to Jamaica and get a job.

2.

razor-gang city

I made the voyage in August 1934, sailing on one of the boats of the Elders and Fyffe steamship line that carried bananas from Jamaica to Britain. It must have been a big family event when that ship left Kingston Harbour. I suppose they thought I would come back but they couldn't have been sure and they would have wondered when they might see me again. In fact, I didn't go back to Jamaica after that for thirty years, and I never saw my father again. It was a real parting of the ways and all the family must have been on the quay. But the details have all gone from my memory. Perhaps, at that time, I put the past out of mind as much as possible because I was always looking forward then. I knew I had to make a go of things, whatever happened and however difficult life became.

It was a long voyage – two weeks – but I had my own cabin and the trip was pleasant. Two of my school pals were on the ship, also coming to study in Britain. I remember arriving in Avonmouth, the port of Bristol, and, before that, passing a sort of green island which I thought looked beautiful. That was Ireland.

When the boat docked and we disembarked down the

gangplank the first thing my feet touched were cobble-stones. Cobbles! That was a terrible shock. You didn't expect to be coming to the mother country from Jamaica and landing on rough cobbles. I thought there should have been a lovely landing stage, a proper welcome for the ship and all that sort of thing. But those ruddy cobbles were the first bit of Britain to make contact with. I hobbled about on them, trying to walk on the uneven surface, carrying my luggage, feeling confused. And then it was a matter of getting to the railway station to find the train to London.

No-one was there to meet me, but some instructions had been written out for me before I left home. My parents must have made inquiries and got help from contacts over here so I would know what to do on arrival. But everything seemed a huge disappointment. On the London train there were no vacant seats. I had to stand the whole way. All this was not at all what I had had in mind. I thought the mother country would have the best of everything. Everything should be pukka.

My instructions were to go to London and find the Young Men's Christian Association which provided hostel accommodation for newcomers to the city. The YMCA building then was more or less where it still is today, near Tottenham Court Road in the West End, and I stayed there for a short while and then moved for a week to lodgings in south London which the YMCA must have arranged.

I don't have strong memories of London at that time. I suppose I was so taken up with the things that had to be done. I spent my time in London getting organised to live in a strange country. As soon as I could, I travelled on by train to the ultimate destination, Glasgow. I had an address to find there and took a taxi from the station.

Then it was time for another big shock. From the back of the taxi I had my first view of Glasgow streets. On both sides were vast, dark, grey stone tenement blocks. There had been nothing like them in Jamaica and I hadn't seen anything in London to make me aware of what their purpose was. What we drove alongside seemed to be just huge walls that blotted out the sky. But I noticed, at the base of the walls, small black holes large enough for people to go through. I sat in the taxi, thinking, 'Where do people live here? I can't see any houses.' Not for a moment did I think that it might be in those little holes. Finally, the taxi stopped alongside a block and the driver called to me, 'Here you are, this is it. Just go through there,' pointing to a hole in the wall.

The block was near City Road, in the heart of the city not far from Sauchiehall Street and the Charing Cross area where there was a popular dance hall. A few years later that would be one of the first places I played professionally. To get into those tenements you had to go along the dark passageway from the road – the hole in the wall, which they called a 'close' – and there would be flights of stairs leading from the close to the flats in the block. I left the taxi, went down the close the driver had pointed out and found the right set of stairs. I was to lodge with a Mr. and Mrs. Rennie and when I arrived they were waiting to greet me at the top of the stairs.

They were a kindly, quite elderly couple. Mrs. Rennie certainly took care of me as well as she could. I didn't become part of their family, or anything as close as that. But she cared and that helped because, of course, I was desperately homesick. It was all such a big change. The Rennies were in the Salvation Army. She was a captain and her husband was a major. They had no children and, apart from Sally Army activities, lived a quiet life. Most people who came to visit were from the Army and they seemed to have few friends outside the organisation. They lived their lives around it and talk in the house was mainly about Sally Army matters.

I had my own room and didn't spend much time with the

Rennies but every so often I would go with them to Army meetings. In a way it was expected. Fortunately, one of the Army people I met, a Miss Carmichael, was very attractive, a really pretty lady. That made those gatherings a lot more interesting. She wasn't a girl friend, or anything like that, but she was very charming. She was quite senior in the local organisation and conducted the meetings.

There were so many new things to get used to and it was really hard. Even the language was difficult at first. For a Jamaican, the Glasgow accent and idiom were very hard to understand. And I had to get used to managing my own money which I had never had to do at home. My parents had taken care of everything. Food was a problem, too. I had to have my meals with the Rennies and they ate a lot of meat, especially lamb. I had never tasted lamb before and hated it. In Jamaica we were used to something completely different. We had goats and ate goat meat. 'I've got to get used to this,' I thought. 'This is what people eat here.' But I hated the powerful aroma of lamb. In the end I couldn't bring myself to eat that meat. Mrs. Rennie was upset about it and I can't remember what she served up instead – probably sausages.

Everything was difficult. You had to make the best you could of it and try to learn new ways and adapt to them. It was dreadful sometimes but you just had to get on with it. Discipline was the answer and my father was a big influence in that. I kept thinking that he had had to do something like this in his time. He had had to apply himself to the task in hand, make his own way, and not let anything deter him. Despite everything, there was never any question of giving up and going back to Jamaica. I couldn't, there was no way. Having come to do something here I had to take life as best I could.

There was very heavy pressure on me to succeed. After all,

my parents were making a big sacrifice. It wasn't cheap to send someone to study in Britain. It cost more money than they could really afford and it was unusual then for anyone to come from Jamaica to study at university in Britain. Occasionally, the schools awarded scholarships and some people came over on those to study but it was very rare to come if you weren't a scholarship holder. So I tried hard to settle in and become a good, dedicated student as quickly as possible.

I didn't have sufficient qualifications to go straight in as an undergraduate at Glasgow University. In those days you had to go to the Royal Technical College nearby, which has now become Strathclyde University, to prepare for the degree course. There was an International Club at the college for students from all over the world, but mostly from various parts of the Empire. The Club organised events and I got to know other students that way. There were no other Jamaicans but some came from India and Africa and my best friend was a Nigerian, Afolabe Alakeja from Lagos, who was there with his brothers Ajikwe and Olatunde. They were sons of a chief and Ajikwe, the eldest, must have eventually gone back to take his father's place, but I lost touch with them later when the war was on. There were a couple of South Africans, Maher and Botha, who spoke in harsh Boer accents that were hard to understand. Botha was dark skinned – very sunburnt you could say – which suggested he had an interesting family history. I didn't have much to do with them.

I was in the club table tennis team. In fact, the International Club was really important in all kinds of ways to overcome the sense of isolation. There were two nice girls in the English faculty and I went to a couple of annual students' conferences with them, all the usual student things. Altogether, I was at the college for three years and then, once I had the qualifications I needed, I started at

Glasgow University in the second year of the engineering degree course. With the college course completed it wasn't necessary to do the first year of the degree. In all, I studied for seven years at the college and the university.

Glasgow was bustling, full of traffic and tramcars that ran along all the broad main streets. Just outside the city centre, a short tram ride away, was Clydeside with its shipbuilding yards and all the industrial activity. I went to watch the *Queen Mary* being launched there at the John Brown shipyard. Huge crowds gathered on September 26th 1934 to see the massive three-funnelled ship being slid down the slipway. It had been great news that it was going to be launched and the whole city turned out to see it, the biggest ocean liner that had been built at that time. I mixed in with the crowd and saw the ship slowly moving, then dipping down into the river majestically and steadying and levelling up with all the great mass of water churning violently around it. That was a great day out.

I got to know areas of the city around the college, the university and the digs where I lived. But there were other places it was best to stay well away from. Glasgow was a rough, violent city in parts, with terrible poverty. The two very bad spots were Cowcaddens and the Gorbals. Cowcaddens was more or less at the end of City Road, the long street where I had my digs, and if you were wise you never went into that area. It was where the poorest people lived, in the huge tenement blocks with their dark closes.

There were razor gangs in Glasgow in those days. Razors were the street gangs' chosen weapon and if you were in the wrong neighbourhood you could easily find a razor at your throat. A lot of robbery took place but much of the fighting was between rival gangs fighting for supremacy. Fortunately I never saw any violence on the streets. I was so busy that I kept to what I needed to do and didn't get about much apart from that. Everyday I would travel to the college or the university to classes and then usually be back in my digs studying. But you would hear on the radio or read in the newspapers that something had happened in some part of the city. I didn't see much of the poverty and unemployment either: the people sleeping in doorways. As a student I spent my time in the nicer parts of town around the university and then later when I got into the Glasgow music scene it was the same. The trouble and the worst poverty were mainly in the back areas where the poor people congregated. There were certainly nice parts of town, where my professor lived, for example.

He was George Howe, the professor of electrical engineering. I got to know him personally because he too was a keen musician. Of course I didn't give up violin playing just because I was studying engineering. I joined the university orchestra and found that Professor Howe was also a violinist. We sat next to each other in the orchestra section: I was leader of the second violins and he was my deputy, so it was a nice status reversal when we played. Eventually he invited me to his house to join him and some friends to play chamber music. His deputy at the university was an oboist and the oboist's wife played piano. So I would play at music sessions on Sunday afternoons at Professor Howe's home.

But I started listening to other kinds of music apart from the classical repertoire I had grown up with in Jamaica and which my father had always insisted was the only music worth bothering with. The electrical engineering lectures made me interested in radio – wireless, we called it – and I started hearing music on the Rennies' radio in my digs. I built a crystal set, and later a proper wireless set of my own, and listened to the swing and dance band music that was broadcast regularly. I discovered that people went to dance halls where bands played the kind of music I was hearing on the radio.

Above all, there was Green's Playhouse, with its huge

floor that could accommodate about 4,000 people. At one end of the dance floor was a stage for the main band and at the other the stage for the relief. Sometimes fights would break out on the dance floor and that was a regular thing after people had had plenty to drink. But the place was so enormous that there might be a big brawl, with lots of men involved, going on at one end of the dance floor while, up at the other end, the dancers would be completely unaware of the disturbance. And, of course, the band would play away, just getting on with the job. Green's was where all the well-known visiting orchestras came to play. It was the place for a special night out. You would go there to see the visiting band and that was a big thing in those days. All the good London bands came and I started to hang around there and eventually began meeting musicians.

I bought a gramophone and began collecting records to add to the classical records I'd brought from Jamaica (and which I still have). I bought new releases by Count Basie, Duke Ellington and swing jump bands like the Spirits of Rhythm. I loved the Spirits, a wonderful, lively little group. Teddy Bunn played lovely guitar and there was that high-pitched instrument, the tipple. That was the sort of jazz that first attracted me, with the feeling and swing they generated, but quiet. They didn't need to play loudly. Then there was Louis Jordan whose music got me into the fun side of jazz. Much later, when I was with Ray Ellington's quartet it seemed entirely natural to bring that side of things out.

Gradually, studying engineering by day and playing classical music at weekends for fun, I began to wonder whether there might, after all, be a way to make a career as a musician and perhaps play this glorious, swinging kind of music I had discovered. There were a few great jazz violinists like Stuff Smith and Joe Venuti but I had a classical technique. Although I wanted to play jazz, I found it impossible on the violin. The classical technique inhibits one's feelings for the value of notes and the way of playing jazz is entirely different. I would have had to grow up in an atmosphere of popular music and jazz improvising while studying the violin classically in order to be able to do both things. Stéphane Grappelli – whom I worked with regularly years later – was the greatest example of that. Stéphane was absolutely wonderful and he had had the opportunity to learn how to do it from an early age. But very few classically trained violinists ever play jazz like a jazz person.

I've always loved the bass line in music. That's why I enjoy Bach so much – the way his bass lines move through a composition. When I first heard the Basie Orchestra I listened to Walter Page, Basie's bassist, and thought that what he was doing was magnificent. That great Basie rhythm section was like a well-oiled machine, swinging so powerfully with Freddie Green on guitar, Jo Jones at the drums and Walter. He had the right idea of how to play a moving bass – a walking bass as it was then called – in a different way from the tonic-dominant style that most bass players followed at that time. Listening to this music and wanting to be able to play it, I thought that since I had learnt violin, maybe I could switch relatively easily to the double bass. After all, it would be the same kind of stringed instrument, just much bigger, and with the musical experience I had, I might learn quite quickly to play the bass and start afresh with a completely new outlook and get into jazz.

When I decided that was what I wanted to do with my life it spurred me to work very very hard. I practised regularly, eight hours a day, and drove Mrs. Rennie mad with it. Other studies eventually got left far behind. But I felt I had to make sure I was capable of mastering this instrument. I had to be able to play it properly and that would take a lot of dedication. The bass I learned on is the fine old instrument I still use today. I've had other basses but this is still my favourite. I love it. It means everything to me. I didn't try playing bass at all before I bought the instrument and, in a way, it was an act of faith getting it. I just decided to give it a try and do my best with it.

Green's Playhouse was a regular haunt once I'd thought seriously about getting into music. I went there all the time after I decided to become a professional. A Sunday jazz club called the Queen Mary started and guys who came to play at Green's would often go along to play jazz at this club as well. It was through one of them, Arthur O'Neill, who came up from London, that I got the bass.

One Sunday he was playing at the Queen Mary and left his bass for a while while he was getting a drink. There was a fireplace with an open fire and Arthur left the instrument too close to the fire, so the back of it got scorched and the varnish melted. But that wasn't the reason he sold it. In fact he hadn't looked after it well and it was in poor condition. From what I could hear of it, however, it sounded nice despite its condition so I made him an offer and he agreed to sell. It was and is a good instrument, made in Mittenwalde in 1860. I took it to the local bass dealers, Briggs and Bryant, to have it repaired and they told me its age and origin. I used to carry it around Glasgow on the trams. One time, as I was standing on a tram platform with it, going to a session at the Queen Mary, the tram swept round a curve in the track and the bass flew out of my hands and smashed on to the road, breaking its neck. It was repaired but eventually it had to have a bolt fitted. Another time many years later in London, a microphone fell into it and smashed the front. So it's seen action.

I would hang around all the places where bands played and try to pick up tips about playing. One was the Locarno Ballroom. A bass player named Bob Smith who came from Newcastle worked with the regular band there. I had heard and watched bass players in various bands and realised that Bob Smith was one who could really play properly. In fact, at that time a lot of bass players in the bands couldn't. They didn't know the instrument thoroughly and just made the sort of adequate noise that was expected from the bass then. Bob turned out to be a very nice chap and very helpful. I'm eternally grateful to him because he put me on the right path, giving me lessons to start with and the right books to study and play from. Unfortunately he's no longer alive but I owe him everything.

All sorts of interesting musicians came through town to play, mainly at Green's. The Oscar Rabin Orchestra was one of the nationally popular dance bands at the beginning of the war. They played an engagement at Green's and I met Oscar's alto player, Harry Conn, who came to my digs. Harry was very into Billie Holiday at the time and played me some of her records, which were just beginning to appear. She soon became one of my great favourites too and I collected all her records as they came out. I bought Jimmy Lunceford records, as well – what a band that was! I wore out my copies of "Tain't What You Do' and 'Four or Five Times' with their Sy Oliver vocals. Then there was all the great music from Ellington, Basie and Django Reinhardt. And Ella Fitzgerald's 'A-Tisket, A-Tasket', which became her first big hit. I still have those old 78 rpm shellacs filed with their faded brown index cards.

Along with the records, the people I heard and saw playing influenced and encouraged me. Norman Stenfalt was the pianist with Rabin around that time and I met him in Glasgow. Later he became a stylish modern jazz player. There was also the alto player Wally Stott, who later became a well known orchestra leader and arranger for the BBC before emigrating to the States. One of the very first visitors I got to know was the pianist/vocalist Cab Kaye, a black entertainer who was in the Merchant Navy and later moved to Holland. His daughter Terri Quaye is a fine conga-player.

There were good local musicians around as well. A drummer, Bobby Foley, was a wonderful player, in fact the best on brushes in the country then. Later, after I moved to London, I persuaded him to come from Glasgow to play at a little club near Marble Arch in a group with guitarist Frank Deniz, Frank's wife Clare on piano, saxophonist Bertie King, and myself on bass. But Bobby was so attached to his mother that he couldn't bear to leave her for long. He lasted maybe three weeks in London and then went back to Glasgow to look after her.

It was a tough city and, of course, there was plenty of racial prejudice and there were reactions as you walked along the street. People of my colour were called darkies then. A mother might be walking along with her children and the children would call out, 'Look momma, look, a darkie!' It was uncommon then to come across black people on the streets. There were very few living in Glasgow. I had my own life at the university and then eventually in the music world and I knew how to deal with prejudice on the streets. After all, I'd had a bit of education. But it wasn't pleasant. The people who did that didn't know any better. They were just ignorant and there was nothing you could do about it. I was always pretty self-reliant. That was what I learned from my father. He had to do everything himself. *Everything.* So I knew it was possible to deal with problems as they arose.

While I was a student I took the opportunity to see some of Britain. Being used to having a motorbike, I bought one in Glasgow. I made friends with an Edinburgh University student, Harihar Pershad, a turban-wearing Sikh, and the two of us set off one summer touring the country from Lands End to John O'Groats for a couple of weeks on this little bike, loaded down with panier bags. So I soon got to know a bit about Britain.

It was a busy full life around the university and then later around the local music scene. As I progressed with the bass, some work started to come through and my first regular job was at the ballroom at Charing Cross not far from my digs.

From the beginning I played bass differently from most of the regular players. For one thing, I liked to use the bow. After all, I was used to bowing a violin and, like the violin, the bass is made to be bowed. From the time I started playing solos I preferred to bow them. I was influenced by Slam Stewart who was attracting attention around 1938 in the 'Slim and Slam' duo with guitarist Slim Gaillard, and also by Wilson Myers, who sometimes used to bow when he played with the Spirits of Rhythm in the 1930s. Slam Stewart had a distinctive way of humming as he bowed his solos and I liked that, although I did it in a different way from him. When you play bass in the section you're generally plucking, of course, playing pizzicato. So it gives a completely different sound when you switch to the bow for a solo. That's what I wanted. And the humming strengthens the sound and creates new possibilities. When I was forming my style I listened carefully to everything that was going on in music, chose what I wanted to do and set out to try to learn how to do it.

So in those Glasgow years I changed direction completely. I've never lost my great love of classical music but I started to map out a future for myself in jazz. The idea of an engineering career was left behind. I did my final thesis for the degree and got a mark of 80%. But by then it was clear that I was going in a completely different direction from the university course. So I never took my final examinations. I was already working as a musician by then.

My parents, of course, didn't know about all this for some

time. They knew I was involved with music, but certainly not jazz. Jazz would have horrified my father. As far as he knew I was playing the violin when I wasn't studying. Dr. Whittaker, his correspondence partner, conducted the university orchestra and must have been very much a symbol of everything George Goode thought of as the real musical world. Despite playing in the orchestra I never got to know Dr Whittaker. He was a busy man. Amongst many other things, he ran the Glasgow Orpheus Choir and was head of the Scottish National Academy of Music. I remember him as a big, full-faced man with wild, flowing locks of grey hair that flew in all directions as he conducted. But perhaps my father thought I was under his musical wing in some way in Glasgow.

My father knew nothing about jazz but he would have got ideas about it from the cinema. Playing jazz was something he would have thought absolutely dreadful. So I kept what I was doing secret. I've never been a very good correspondent but I wrote to my mother occasionally and she would relay news to him. For a long time they did not know what I was really aiming at for my career but when my mother found out she was very supportive. Until I had proven myself, however, I needed to keep everything away from my father. I felt that was necessary until he could begin to recognise that I wasn't wasting my life. When he did eventually discover I was working as a jazz musician he was very disappointed indeed. He was totally disapproving and there was no correspondence between the two of us. Eventually he changed his mind, once he saw the success of the Ray Ellington Quartet which I was with in the late 1940s. The news about that reached him and I think he was pleased. He felt better about it because at least I had succeeded in something.

In the end, although he would never have approved of jazz, he would have been glad I was playing music and that

I was recognised by people as doing it well. The important thing isn't so much what you do as how you do it. In some families you have to be a doctor or lawyer, one of the respectable professions, if you are going to be 'somebody'. But that's not the case generally now. What is important is to recognise the talents that you were given when you were put on this earth and if you develop those properly that's all right. Thank God for that.

It's the course I followed with my children. Find out what they are good at, what it is they enjoy doing and then let them do that for the rest of their lives, because to do something that you don't enjoy when times are hard is like purgatory. If your work is something you really want to do and you enjoy it, when the times get hard you put up with the difficulties. And the profession of music is a hard profession. My son Jim is an actor and he also plays music a bit. He has a good musical sense but I didn't press him to go into the music business because he had a really good talent as an actor.

Of course, there was no opportunity to discuss things face to face with my father. I didn't go back and he didn't come here. Some years after I left Jamaica he retired from the civil service and went to live at a place called Half Way Tree, one of the nice areas then, in another part of St. Andrew. He died in 1963 and it was only the year after that when I went back to Jamaica for the first time. At the memorial service for him in October 1963 in St. Michael's Church, the Jamaica Philharmonic Symphony Orchestra and the Diocesan Festival Choir took part in the programme. Part of Bach's 'Sleepers, Wake', the piece he asked Dr. Whittaker's advice about all those years before, was included. I did see my mother after I moved to Britain. She visited for a month in 1956, and then again after my father had died.

***

Altogether, I lived in Glasgow for seven years but I never put down any roots there. As the lure of becoming a professional musician grew stronger it was obviously important to move to London. That was the best place for musical advancement. One thing that gave a final push happened when the Oscar Rabin band made one of its occasional visits to play for a week or two at Green's. A tenor player in the band, George Roberts, a fine musician, went off with my girlfriend. She followed him back to London and I was very cut up about it. So I didn't think anything was keeping me in Glasgow.

Sometime early in 1941 I decided to contact Ken Johnson who led the band at the Café de Paris, a very plush and exclusive London dining and dancing club off Leicester Square. Ken was a dancer (nicknamed 'Snake Hips') who had come originally from Guyana (then British Guiana). He had a very successful group, sometimes called the West Indian Orchestra, made up of some of the top black musicians in the country. It had toured, recorded and broadcast, had a big reputation and had held the prestigious Café de Paris residency for a couple of years. I thought that it would certainly be the best band to join and that I was ready for it. For me it was *the* band, the biggest inspiration at the time. So I wrote to Ken Johnson to see if he might need a bass player. But no reply came to my letter.

By then the wartime Blitz was well under way. London was being bombed every night and other cities too. It was something everyone had to put out of their mind as much as they could, otherwise it would have been impossible to carry on with everyday life. But even if I had had a reply to my letter to Ken Johnson the Blitz would have put an end to any further possibilities of a musical relationship with him. On March 8th 1941, he was killed outright when a German bomb fell on the Café de Paris in an air raid and reduced the place to rubble while his band was playing there. Several musicians and a lot of other people died in the blast.

In Glasgow I was working regularly with the band at the Charing Cross dance hall and on Sundays I would be playing jazz at the Queen Mary Club. I carried on with that for some time but eventually decided to make a trip to London to see for myself what the music scene was like. I arrived in the city early in 1942 and looked around for a few days visiting places where music was played. By then the worst of the nightly Blitz bombing was over so it was possible to get around and there were a lot of places where you could hear music.

Eventually, I found myself in a small club where a pianist I didn't know had the regular gig. I didn't really know *anybody* at the time, but I had taken along my bass so he let me sit in and we played a few things as a duo. His name was Dick Katz and I asked whether he knew of any places where it might be possible to get work. He had heard about a club that was just about to open and gave me the details. I went along and got the job straight away. I thought, 'Right, that's got to be it. I'll move down here.' So I dashed back to Glasgow, packed all my things together and left. I set off for London with no idea what the future might bring (or that a few years later Dick Katz would have a big part in it). It seemed the most exciting thing to be taking fate with both hands and going for whatever the big city had to offer.

3.

from the Panama to the Caribbean Club

Things happened quickly after I arrived in London in the spring of 1942. I started at the club Dick Katz had mentioned, working with a five piece group. One evening in the very first week, someone familiar, a dapper man in his mid-twenties, came in to the club, settled himself at the bar, and spent some time listening to the music we were playing. His name was Johnny Claes. I knew his face because I had seen him in Glasgow playing trumpet with a band at Barrowlands, a dance hall where a lot of the visiting groups went even though it was in one of the more unsavoury parts of town. At the time I heard Johnny playing in Glasgow, I was also impressed with other members of the band he was with – another trumpeter, Duncan Whyte, for example, and the wonderful saxophonist Bertie King, whom I would work with in later years.

It turned out that Johnny Claes was noticing me, too. He was part Belgian and had divided his career up to then between Britain and the Continent. He had worked recently in Brussels for his father's business as well as playing music, but in 1940, just before the Nazis moved in to Belgium, he returned to Britain and toured with Teddy

Joyce's orchestra. That may have been the band that came to Barrowlands. Now Johnny had a band of his own, called the 'Claepigeons'. He must have liked my playing that evening because, at some point, he came up to me and asked me whether I'd like to join his band.

I said yes immediately. I knew he was a fine jazz player and had no doubts. In fact, the Claepigeons were *the* small jazz group in London at that time. Not many bands really played jazz then. There were plenty of dance bands where the jazz soloists were allowed to take a hot chorus or two once in a while if they were lucky. Otherwise they could only play jazz informally and for little or no money in small clubs after their work in the dance halls or restaurants was over for the night. But Johnny's band played jazz as much as possible and dressed up their show with entertainment to make a good cabaret.

The band varied in size but usually there was a five-piece front line – four saxes plus Johnny's trumpet, which he played in a brassy Roy Eldridge style. His big sound was always right out in front. The band personnel was always changing and a lot of musicians who passed through became well-known names in British jazz. In fact, Claes is probably best remembered now for the fact that Ronnie Scott got his start with him. But that was a few years later.

Among the musicians when I was there was the tenor sax-ophonist Kenny Graham. Kenny, who later led a wonderful Afro-Cuban band, was trying to avoid military service and disguised himself during his time with the Claepigeons under the name of Tex Kershaw. He was a hard-blowing player, efficient, with a nice sound and he was very extro-vert, a devil-may-care type of character. In fact, they were all like that. The baritone player, Derek Neville, a very fat guy, had a car with the words 'It's a Bugger!' painted right across it. The war got rid of all the stuffiness. People were down-to-earth or they just didn't care.

When I first joined, Tommy Pollard was the pianist. He was a big, well-built chap with a flourishing, powerful style. Bernie Fenton, who was very competent on piano and also did some arranging, soon took over. Johnny's girlfriend Billie Campbell sang and later, after she left, there was a black girl singer whom Bernie took a shine to so that they became partners.

Through the whole time I was with the Claepigeons, the regular drummer was Carlo Krahmer, a very dynamic character on the London jazz scene in the war years. He was into everything and eventually ran several bands of his own and set up a record label, Esquire, which became very important in documenting modern jazz in Britain. Carlo was practically blind, with just a tiny bit of sight left, and always a quiet person. Not being able to see he would listen very intently all the time. But despite his disability he lugged his drums all over London through the Blitz. He rushed around at great speed to get from one band to another, because he often had several things on the go at any one time. He would take the lighter bits of his equipment with him on the underground, tucking his cymbals under his arm and he would leave a bass drum wherever he was most regularly working at the time. Carlo had a slightly military style of drumming. He sat in a very upright posture and played in a deliberate way, using the cymbals much more than other drummers did then. He certainly had his own style.

It wasn't just Carlo who lugged his instrument around on the tube. I travelled that way too. In fact, during the war, the underground was often the safest way of getting around. In mid-1942 while I was with the Claes band, it had a residency at the Panama Club, near Knightsbridge tube station, not far from Harrods department store.

I didn't spend much time socialising with the other

musicians. We would do the job at the Panama each night
and then get home or wherever we were going as quickly as
possible. You didn't hang around when there could be air
raids and anything might happen. While you were working
you never knew what might be going on outside. It was a
fleeting existence for everyone in those war years.
Musicians came in and out of the dozens of bands that
played the London clubs and everything was totally uncertain, so people took things as they came.

I didn't cement any huge friendships at the time. Everyone was concerned with doing the job and getting away
safely. Also, it was a time when I was still trying to tame this
instrument I'd taken up and get myself as much technique
as possible. So I spent a lot of time practising. But I did
sometimes go along to Archer Street, the traditional place
where the musicians met during the day, crowding the pavement, exchanging gossip and fixing up gigs. I had regular
work so I wasn't looking for jobs but I would go down there
once in a while just to pick up a bit of news and see who was
around.

The Panama was a drinking club with only a small dance
floor. We were there to entertain the people and not specially to play for dancing. So the music was swing style with
a high jazz content, jump band kind of stuff with some high
notes here and there. Johnny was always a good showman.
He dressed nattily with a white handkerchief in the sleeve
of his jacket and his hair neat and well brushed back.
Between the jazz sets there was a cabaret which involved
the band with special musicians and other artistes added.

The showman *par excellence* was a black vaudeville
American drummer called Freddie Crump. Although Carlo
was the regular drummer, Freddie played in the cabaret. He
was a tremendous character, very loud and powerful but –
my goodness! – the tricks he did. He had a very fast right
foot on the bass drum pedal and played fast on the cymbals.

And he would really throw the sticks around. His act would end with him springing off the drums on to the floor in front of the drumkit. Freddie was a special feature, and everyone loved that bit of the show.

The place where we worked was what we called then a 'day club' in contrast to a night club. In day clubs work would start around 8.00 pm and finish at perhaps 11.00 pm and then you might go on somewhere else to play. I badly needed the money at that time so as soon as the Panama closed for the night I would go on to another club called the Slip In, off Regent Street on the right hand side going up towards Oxford Circus. That was a real night club. The music would start around midnight and go on until three or four in the morning. When I first came to London I would work like that every night because it was the only way to earn a living. When you're young and strong you can do it. At the Panama I was earning about eight pounds a week and that was good pay in those days.

The Panama wasn't the top but it was decent. The clientele were the well-heeled people who lived around Knightsbridge. The Slip In was just the opposite. It was a haunt of gangster types. When the honest, decent people were in bed these other characters would come out to have their fun and drink their way through the night. And they were usually big tippers. One prominent patron at the Slip In was a really notorious gangster and, of course, we played things we knew he would like. He would sometimes ask us to play particular tunes and we always went along with his requests.

Not all the musicians from the Claes band would go on from the Panama to the Slip In but, if anyone is going on to play, of course the bass player has to go. You always have to have a bass. So I would take the instrument by tube. Then, after the music had finished at the Slip In I'd go on to the old Lyons Corner House, between Leicester Square and

Piccadilly. It stayed open all night and all the musicians would meet up there at about five o'clock in the morning. We'd gossip together and drink coffee until the dawn broke.

Then I would go back to my lodgings. At first, I lived in West Hampstead at Una Marson's flat. She was the sister of my father's secretary Ethel Marson, so that was the connection I had. Una worked for the BBC, producing radio programmes broadcast from London to the West Indies. They were done mainly so that the families, in Jamaica and elsewhere, of servicemen fighting in the war could hear messages from their loved ones, broadcast as part of a show with popular songs, calypsos and swing music. Una lived not far from Shoot Up Hill and somehow or other I had found that out and got in touch with her and she put me up. I remember at least two occasions when I took some of the band back there to sleep on the floor.

Most of the time with Johnny Claes was spent working in London clubs. A lot of them were thriving because London was full of servicemen out to enjoy themselves and trying to forget the war for a few hours. But I didn't see much of club life really, because the regular jobs we had at a few places like the Panama and the Slip In – and later the Embassy Club, a plush night club on Bond Street – filled almost every night. Although most work was in London we did a few out of town engagements including a week at the Theatre Royal, Chatham, in May 1942 and we made at least one armed services broadcast for the BBC that same month, probably for Una's West Indies programme.

After that, the band was booked for a tour of American forces bases in England through the end of September and early October. That wasn't the only time I did that sort of work for the forces. I also toured the bases with a show put together by Bebe and Ben Lyons, the American comedy stars. It was expected at the time, part of the war effort, and everyone had to contribute somehow. But the Claes tour turned out to be memorable for all the wrong reasons. In fact some things that happened on that tour left a permanent mark on me – and not just on me.

At the end of June 1942, a guitarist named Lauderic Caton had joined the band. Lauderic soon became a close friend. He was a wonderful soloist, with an original style and endless musical imagination. And he was a very sensitive, rather withdrawn and serious person. I remember he wrote a piece for Johnny called 'Swinging on a Rusty Gate'. Later I worked with him a lot, but the Claepigeons was our first job together. We were the only two black musicians in the band at that time, and Lauderic had come from Trinidad originally so there was a strong West Indian connection between us. He had worked in Martinique and reached London in 1940, via jobs in France and Belgium. And he had been with clarinettist Harry Parry's sextet just before he joined Johnny.

The Claes band got as far as Bristol on the American forces tour and we were all booked in to a hotel there. When we arrived the hotel management decided that they wouldn't allow Lauderic and myself to stay. Johnny Claes was furious. The whole band walked out and we all went back to the place where we had been playing the night before and stayed there. The reason for what happened at the hotel was probably the big influence of the Americans in Bristol at that time. The hotel would have been enjoying a lot of American custom then from servicemen and they were obviously trying to keep them happy by pandering to the racist attitudes the GIs brought over with them.

That wasn't all. Something similar happened on another occasion during the tour when we were playing at one of the American bases and the band had its break between sets. We all went for a meal on the base and the white guys from the band were put to sit at a table in one room and

Lauderic and I were put at a different table in a different room. Lauderic was so fed up that he just left the base there and then and went home. He got up without saying anything much and left the band and went straight back to London. If he didn't like a situation and it really upset him he had a tendency to get up and go. I saw it happen again with him, in a different way, some years after. But that's something to tell later. Certainly what happened on that tour helped to disillusion him in all sorts of ways that became more pronounced over time.

I saw plenty of that kind of racism from the American forces during the war. Fights would often break out when black servicemen tried to dance or talk with English girls in clubs or dance halls. The white GIs would start a brawl when they saw the black servicemen with the girls. I saw all that kind of nastiness. Those poor guys were humiliated so often. It was terrible. Sometimes things were so bad that the American authorities in Britain designated some pubs and clubs as either 'white' or 'black' so that only white GIs were allowed to go to some and only black ones to others. That way the authorities tried to prevent the troops from mixing, because it so often led to trouble if they did. All this made me think about these attitudes, all that vileness, which the Americans brought over here and about what it would be like to live in America. I decided I couldn't ever live there. I couldn't have taken all that vicious, racist behaviour. No self-respecting person could. I would probably have ended up killing someone or being killed.

Later on in my career these reactions that formed in my mind became decisive because some people suggested to me at various times that I might do well over there in the States. They would say, 'You should go to America. It would be really good for your career. That's the place to make it as a jazz musician.' But I was very sure that I wouldn't go. In fact, I never really have spent any time there. I stopped

over in New York once, years after the war, on the way to
visit Jamaica. I went to Birdland and the Five Spot, just to
see where those famous jazz clubs were. It was on the route,
in a way. But I've never wanted to spend any more time
there. I saw enough during the war.

In October 1942, soon after the end of that short tour,
Johnny disbanded the Claepigeons. He reformed later and
led bands throughout the war years but it was the end of
my association with him. When the war ended he went
back to Brussels and the family business, got married and
ran a jazz club in Blankenberge. Eventually he gave up playing trumpet and turned seriously to motor racing but he
died of cancer before he reached his forties.

Just as the period with the Claepigeons came to an end,
Eric Winstone was looking for a bassist and asked me to
join him. He played the accordion and had a little band,
doing novelty numbers, songs and tunes he wrote himself,
and ballads. He had probably heard about me through the
'guitar connection' with Lauderic Caton: Lauderic knew the
Deniz brothers, who were also guitarists. Frank Deniz
worked with Winstone and would have known about me
when Eric's need for a bass player came up. As well as Eric
on squeeze box and Frank on guitar, there was Roy Marsh
on vibraphone, and occasionally drums and piano, and an
attractive singer named Julie Dawn. The music wasn't jazz
as we know it but it was lively. It was just a musical act that
the quintet did, putting on a stage show in the theatres for
listeners rather than dancers. The first date I did with them
was a Saturday concert in Chatham on November 21st 1942.
Then we played a week at the naval base there.

Roy Marsh was a good player but Eric was just standard.
One thing he became known for was a piece he wrote called
'Stagecoach', which became his signature tune. He had a
nervous affliction of some kind and every so often would

have to thump himself violently to get it under control and pump his finger and make grotesque faces. All this was very strange but it didn't stop him playing. Sometimes it would happen on stage, but it was a bit more under control then. No-one bothered. I suppose in wartime people expect anything.

I wasn't close to Eric as a person. No-one ever hobnobbed with the bandleaders in those days. They had their own set of people that they moved around with, but I think he was always pretty close to Roy Marsh. They had worked together for years. For me it was always just a question of doing the job. We travelled a lot, doing a week here and a week there, and if you stay in digs but not in the same digs as the others you don't socialise a lot off the bandstand. You come to the show, do it and then part company. With Eric Winstone we usually had an elaborate stage presentation to put on, so I would go to the theatre for rehearsals and after that we would do the show.

Julie Dawn had a lovely soprano voice. She was a very voluptuous lady and a sweet person. She came from an Italian family and could sing in several languages, and she was featured with the big band that Eric Winstone also ran. I played in that too but only for recording sessions for Regal Zonophone and the records were very popular. The big band always had the cream of musicians. Harry Hayes, the altoist, was one. Above all, there was Carl Barriteau who had come from Trinidad and was certainly the finest clarinet player around at that time.

He had been in Ken Johnson's band and had been injured when the German bomb hit the Café de Paris in 1941. Later, after his time with Eric, Carl was a bandleader in his own right and became very famous. I played with him occasionally in later years. The last time was a fortnight in Edinburgh when he had a group about the same size as the Claepigeons. He played various reeds but clarinet was his speciality and he really was a master of it. Carl married the singer Mae Cooper and when they emigrated to Australia, many years later, she worked with him in a cabaret act they shared. She was a great solace and strength to him.

During the time I was with Eric Winstone, my domestic situation changed fundamentally. I had been living at Una Marson's house but, of course, it wasn't a perfect arrangement. I didn't want to impose on her so I looked around for somewhere else after a time. One night after work I went to a drinking club and got talking to a young lady. It turned out that she had a house in Hampstead with a spare room and eventually I moved in there. She was an Austrian, named Herta Nott. Her parents were rich and had given her this house in London. After I had moved in, one of Herta's old school friends from Vienna, whose family was of Hungarian origin, got in touch with her and came to visit. I was away touring somewhere with Eric at the time and Herta put up her friend in my bed in the spare room. So when I got back I met the friend and we got along very well. Her name was Gertrude Selmeczi and before long we were a couple. It didn't take long for me to know I wanted to make it permanent and after six months or so we decided we knew each other well enough. So on January 26th 1944 we turned up at the Town Hall in Hampstead and were duly married. We have been ever since.

I stayed with Winstone until early 1944 but in March of that year the Jamaican trumpeter, Leslie 'Jiver' Hutchinson, formed a band and I decided to join that. It started out with a lot of high expectations. When Jiver left Geraldo's orchestra to form 'Leslie 'Jiver' Hutchinson and His All-Coloured Band', *Melody Maker* announced it as 'the most sensational piece of news this week in the dance band world.' He had been Geraldo's star trumpet soloist, so he had a very big name. He had a good tone and a good big sound and a lot of the outstanding West Indian players joined the new orchestra: Dave Wilkins on trumpet, Bertie King and George Roberts among the saxes, pianist Yorke de Sousa who later became my long-time tennis partner, Joe Deniz on guitar and drummer Clinton Maxwell. Bert Ambrose promoted the new project, fixed up bookings and promised all kinds of success. But I didn't stay long with that band.

In fact, I don't remember much about it except that it was full of very keen card players. We travelled by train and the card games would start and the money would begin changing hands as soon as the train left the station. I had a push-bike then and I'd take it on the train and cycle around whatever town we were staying in. It was a good way of keeping fit and I had gone back to riding a pushbike because my old motorcycle had been stolen some time before. The motorbike had come with me from Glasgow to London and I had kept it in Herta Nott's garage. But one day it mysteriously disappeared from there and I never saw it again.

There were certainly good players in Jiver's band but it could have been better run and I soon managed to get into other things which were musically much more interesting. So those things have pushed Jiver's music out of my memory.

Sometime in 1944 I started working at a place in Denman Street in Piccadilly called the Caribbean Club and that began one of the most satisfying periods in my career. I played there regularly for three years. The club was run by a chap called Rudy Evans, a Jamaican, whose brother was our family dentist back in Jamaica. Lauderic was playing there with Dick Katz, the pianist who had been the first musician to give me a helping hand when I had moved to London. They needed a bass player and Lauderic suggested

I join them to make up the trio. I already loved Lauderic's playing so I was ready to drop other things I was doing if there was the chance of a regular job with him and Dick in a good club.

In fact, the Caribbean Club was ideal, a wonderful environment. It was fairly small and compact, mid-market and not sleazy. The acoustics were good and the atmosphere was very special. It was a genuinely mixed club in terms of race and class. That was something that made it unusual and successful because most clubs in those days weren't mixed like that. Val Wilmer wrote that at the Caribbean Club, 'Caribbean and African-American officers rubbed shoulders with Whitehall mandarins and aristocracy' and that's how I remember it. There were a lot of West Indians from the various islands who knew each other, and well-known people – artists, actors and celebrities – would drop in. It was very free and easy.

Stairs led up to the club and inside there was a small dance floor, but mainly people came to listen and drink. I didn't drink at all then so I don't remember whether there was a bar. But the usual thing was 'bottle parties' in those days. Everyone would bring in their own bottles, whatever they preferred to drink, and share it around. The club didn't serve food. It was just a place to drink and relax.

Rudy Evans, the proprietor, would sing. He was very partial to French songs like 'J'attendrai', and another of his favourites was 'East of the Sun', so he provided most of the cabaret every night singing with the trio, and the rest of the time Lauderic, Dick Katz and I would provide the music on our own or with occasional guest musicians sitting in. It was homely in a way and most of the clientele were regulars and knew each other well. It was a very good atmosphere and we could do interesting things with the music because we felt completely relaxed playing there.

I loved to play with Lauderic and Dick. We liked to have

an intellectual quality to the music and make it a real contrast to the ordinary popular dance band thing. We were all
good players and could put our own individual taste into
each number so we specialised in playing things that people
didn't hear much in the clubs at that time. We transcribed
a lot of Duke Ellington's compositions for the trio. Dick
was very fond of Ellington's music and could get the kind of
piano sound the Duke did. He was a very solid player,
physically very chunky too, solidly built but a chain smoker
– that's what did for him in the end. When he played he
would pump his leg up and down and bang it on the floor.
So, later, when the trio became well-known and we started
to do broadcasts, he had to have a cushion put under his
foot on the floor to stop the sound. He couldn't play without that.

Like all of us, he had learned his jazz from records, so it's
amazing how beautifully he could interpret Ellington and
produce lovely, original sounds in the different kinds of
things we did. He was Jewish and had grown up in Germany.
When the Nazis came to power, his family fled to Holland
and he came over to Britain around the time war between
Britain and Germany broke out. He was an outstanding
piano player and it's sad that there isn't more of his work on
record.

Dick played very rhythmically and kept an absolutely
strict tempo which, of course, is a definite asset. A lot
of musicians can't keep the tempo and as a bass player
you really feel that. Especially when you don't have a
drummer, it's essential that everyone in the group feels the
beat together. Dick and I made a good team and I'm
grateful for that experience because you discover when you
start playing with some drummers, for example, that it's
hard work because the tempos vary all the time. You can
be sorely tried. You have to carry the drummer and that's
hard because drums are so loud. But with the Caribbean

Trio, as we became known, there was no problem, because everything was balanced beautifully between the three instruments.

We put together intricate arrangements, using all the resources you could get from a piano-guitar-bass trio. And each of us was musically curious and adventurous, in terms of the musical styles of the time. We put all our ideas into the music and tried to make everything fresh with new voicings and textures of sound. My big influence then was Ellington's bass player Jimmy Blanton, who was giving the bass a prominence and subtlety it had never had before in jazz. I made transcriptions of his solos which I still have. I would listen to all the good bass players who came to this country. I'd learn everything I could from them, but then try to do things my own way.

Lauderic was into new things too. He was a complex character, intellectually driven and he talked in a studied, considered way about everything. He was something of a loner in social terms, a real home lover, and that side of him had come out when he had run off and left Johnny Claes a few years before. But he was certainly ambitious for what he wanted to achieve musically. At the beginning of the 1940s the American guitarist Charlie Christian was beginning to develop a completely new style for his instrument – an aggressive, complex solo style with new harmonic ideas – and pointing towards bebop and modern jazz. He made some records with Benny Goodman and everyone noticed this young musician with a new sound. A few years after that, Charlie Parker and Dizzy Gillespie began to develop the new modern jazz style on records, but Charlie Christian was the forerunner and Lauderic had really picked up on that and admired Christian very much. So he worked out a comparable style very different from the other guitarists working in London at that time. Also, Christian was one of the first musicians to play the electric guitar. Amplified guitars were something completely new in the mid-1940s. Lauderic took that up and got himself an American amplifier for his guitar so he could explore all these new ideas that Charlie Christian had come up with.

Like me, he had an aptitude for technological things. You could say he was a bit intellectually gifted, in a Trinidad kind of way – practical and inventive. He studied electronics and built his own television set. In fact, we both did that around the same time. I built my first television set myself. So we had that interest in common. And when Lauderic developed his ideas about amplifying his guitar electrically and experimented with equipment, trying to get the sound he wanted, I started to experiment in a similar way with my bass. Amplification opened up new possibilities for the guitar as a solo instrument and gave it a new kind of place in a jazz group, and I began to think that something similar could apply with the bass.

'If I'm going to play solos, I want to be heard,' I thought. Nowadays that is an obvious idea, but it wasn't then. People tended to say that it was not necessary to hear the bass. You should just be able to feel it. But, as a bass player, you often have to put up with loud drummers and the acoustics in the place where you're playing might not be wonderful. In a large group, what the bass is playing can easily be drowned out by the volume of sound from other instruments and, if you are playing well and really contributing harmonically and rhythmically to the group, a lot is lost if the bass doesn't come through sufficiently. If you're not heard, it's just a lot of work for nothing.

So during 1946, at the Caribbean Club, I experimented with amplification. I tried various kinds of pick-ups on the strings and ultimately found that the best sound came from using pick-ups on the bridge. I've amplified my bass that way ever since. In the early days it was experimental and a bit risky. I once got a massive mains shock touching a microphone and the bass strings at the same time when something had been wired up incorrectly. And a lot of musicians thought amplification was a big mistake, that it would destroy the purity of the bass sound. It was the same sort of criticism that the early players of the electric guitar, like Lauderic Caton, faced. But eventually most people came round to seeing the point of it.

Nevertheless, amplification does cause problems for the bass. I have often found that recording engineers don't know how to record the amplified sound properly. They are used to recording the string sound directly and don't know how to place the microphones in relation to the amplification equipment. Usually, by the time they get to the end of the recording session they've got the sound just about right.

In fact, the Caribbean Trio never did go into a recording studio so the issue didn't arise just then. We did broadcasts for the BBC and some of the music from those was put on disc. But in the period of economic austerity, at the end of the war and just after it, everything had to be done in the cheapest way so the records were made of glass, with just a thin shellac veneer. I kept copies of them but, over the years, the shellac peeled off and the records became completely unplayable. I still have them, but they are useless. So the sound of all those lovely arrangements, the group interplay and Dick and Lauderic's inspired playing on those pieces is lost now.

Just a few performances on record have survived – almost by accident, you could say – of the 'Caribbean Quartet'. The quartet came about because Bertie King sometimes used to work with us at the Caribbean Club and on broadcasts. Other musicians would sit in with the trio sometimes but Bertie guested on a regular basis for a time. Tragically, he is almost forgotten now but he was a lovely saxophone player. With the trio he also doubled on drums, usually brushes, so it made a good, compact group.

He had grown up in Jamaica and he made the move to Britain a year after I did. I first saw and heard him in Glasgow, when he came through from London working alongside Johnny Claes and Duncan Whyte, and he impressed me straight away. Instrumentalists used to throw themselves around a lot in those days when they played, but Bertie would stand absolutely still and all you would see moving would be his fingers on the saxophone keys. He had a most beautiful alto sound with something of Benny Carter and Johnny Hodges in it. He was certainly my favourite alto player on the local scene. He and Harry Hayes were the two outstanding altoists in Britain at that time.

Billed as the Caribbean Quartet we made a radio broadcast for the BBC's 'Jazz Matinée' programme in August 1947. I kept the acetate recordings of the broadcast safely for half a century. Then, recently, a friend made up a CD from them for me, cleaning up the sound in the process. So they are really all there is that can be heard of the group now. Jack Jackson's announcements on the broadcast sound relaxed and humorous, not at all like the usual stilted announcers of the day. The trio, plus Bertie's brushes, plays 'Poinciana' and then Jackson says: 'Now, if Bertie King can extricate himself from his bass drum pedal he's going to play you 'Come Sunday", which he does with hardly any improvising but a rich, romantic, swooping sound with a slight reediness.

On some of the other pieces, the guitar and the alto are so tight in unison and so close in pitch and texture in the theme statements that it sounds like a single instrument playing. Where the trio alone is featured, Bertie can be heard softly backing on drums. On alto, on some of the faster numbers, he plays in a sort of jump style with his angular, slightly hesitant phrasing. There is a version of 'Mr. J. B. Blues', which Ellington and Jimmy Blanton had record-ed as one of their duets. On that, Dick and I are featured and there is a bowed and hummed bass solo. Of course, we played most of these pieces regularly, so it's not surprising that the group sounds tightly rehearsed, with close inter-play, intricate arranged passages and continual shifts in rhythm and textures of sound.

The Caribbean Trio was a highlight of my career. It was the first group I played with in which I felt that I could really express myself fully with my own musical ideas. It existed at a time when change was in the air musically. Around the time the war ended in 1945 new ideas began to be heard on record from America. Bebop was beginning to be the new thing. Lauderic brought some of those ideas in through the Charlie Christian influence and all of us were adjusting our musical thinking in one way or another, though it took me a while to begin to feel and understand the idiom of mod-ern jazz. But there were other things too that were perhaps as important as the music. The Caribbean Club was a kind of ideal of how people could mix without tensions and trou-ble. As the war ended we were looking ahead to the way things might be better.

As for me, I had a home and a family. Gertrude and I found a place to live soon after we married. But as a mixed race couple it certainly wasn't easy to find somewhere. We would see places advertised and go along to look at them, and then it would regularly be a matter of, 'Oh, I'm so sorry, it's just been let.' There never was a chance once I showed my face. That was the way things always were then. It was Rudy Evans, the owner of the Caribbean Club, who put me on to a place in Notting Hill where we could finally settle down – in the house we live in now. He lived a few streets from here and knew the house had been requisitioned by the armed forces but also that part of it was empty. The tenant had gone off to the war. So we were able to move in. I was the second West Indian in the neighbourhood. Rudy was the first.

The place was in a terrible mess. There were cobwebs everywhere and cracks in the ceiling and the walls, because bombs had fallen nearby. But it was somewhere to make our own. In 1945 our daughter Sandy was born and later our son Jim. So I had a family to look after and a home to keep. Fortunately, a lot of new possibilities were waiting around the corner, but for the moment it was a matter of making the best of all the varied musical experiences that came my way. And some turned out to be very special.

4.

Django, Stéphane and friends

During part of the period when I was at the Caribbean Club I also worked regularly with Stéphane Grappelli and George Shearing, doing BBC broadcasts. Stéphane was famous for the wonderful records he had made in the 1930s with Django Reinhardt and the Quintet of the Hot Club of France. After war broke out, Django stayed in France but Stéphane settled himself in London and Britain became effectively his 'other country' which he came to love. He formed a band to play at Hatchett's restaurant in Piccadilly and worked there, on and off, throughout the war years. I never played with him at Hatchett's but he did ask me to join the small group he had for broadcasts. That probably started in 1945.

Stéphane was a wonderful jazz violinist. His facility and accuracy were tremendous and his intonation was perfect. I never heard him play out of tune and he had a subtle approach to notes: he wouldn't hit them right in the middle, but would caress them and draw them out, swooping into them rather like Johnny Hodges' alto sax did at the time with Ellington. George Shearing, who was recognised by everyone as a prodigy, a truly brilliant musician, was the pianist in Stéphane's group at Hatchett's and on the broadcasts.

During the war there were underground cinemas in London, one at Marble Arch and the other in Piccadilly. One was called the Monseigneur. The BBC took them over for broadcasting and that was where we would play. The group didn't broadcast regularly but every so often we would be booked - usually Stéphane, Shearing, Eric Delaney on drums, and me. We would discuss what to do and have a short rehearsal and then the music would go out over the air. I remember that once we were at the studio and Eric had not arrived. We waited and waited and nothing was happening. No-one could get in touch with him. Eventually it turned out that he had not been able to get his car started and had been fiddling about under the bonnet. He had got his fingers entangled in the fan-belt and more or less cut one of them off. It was a dreadful thing to happen and he didn't play with us after that.

Seeing Shearing and Grappelli working together was something special. George, being completely blind, couldn't write anything down and had to have everything in his head. So if he wanted to work something out that we could use – an arrangement or some musical phrases – he would go to the piano and start playing and Grappelli would write it down – the melody line, or the phrases or voicings – there and then and we would play it. Shearing came up with ideas all the time. He was so imaginative. And if Stéphane wanted to play something and show the group what to do, he would only have to do that once and George would have everything clear in his head and remember every detail. Most of what we broadcast must have been things that the two of them played together regularly at Hatchett's but we never used any of the material that Stéphane had recorded with Django in the pre-war days of the Hot Club. He had moved on to new things by then.

Grappelli and Shearing would decide between them what we were going to play, with Shearing's dry, often black humour sometimes much in evidence and Stéphane explaining what he had in mind in that very French English he had, laced with expressive French phrases and with his strong French accent. He was very soft in his manner and he spoke quietly, in a sort of mincing way. I never had any social life with him and we just met to play. But he certainly loved to do that and, although he had had formal tuition on the violin, he played against the rules, very much in his own way. As someone who had learned classical violin, I appreciated that. Grappelli was always happy when he was playing. And at the broadcasts he would always have a little something with him for refreshment, stashed away in his violin case. Usually a bottle of good cognac. He loved his tipple.

I didn't have much contact with Shearing either, apart from when we actually played. He was so obviously outstanding that he was a very busy person, much in demand. His wife Trixie would always be around, ready to whisk him off to wherever he next needed to be. So we didn't talk much. But when he decided finally to emigrate to the States it wasn't a big surprise. It was something that seemed to be very much on the cards given his enormous talent. There were quite a few musicians immediately after the war who thought seriously about moving to America and some did, because they decided they were good enough and felt drawn to the States. The pianist Ralph Sharon was one who went and he became Tony Bennett's accompanist for many years. So when Shearing emigrated in 1947 it seemed a natural move for him.

One night, some time after I had begun doing the broadcasts with Stéphane Grappelli, I was playing at the Caribbean Club with the trio when a strange figure walked in. He was wearing huge boots, like mountain boots, and looked as though he had just returned from climbing an alpine peak. All of us on the bandstand recognised him straight away. It was Django Reinhardt – the legendary Django. I don't think I even knew that he was in London at the time. He came up to the bandstand when we had finished playing a piece, and had a look at the guitar Lauderic Caton was using. Lauderic had had the neck of his guitar widened. Perhaps that was what Charlie Christian had done with his, I'm not sure. But Django saw this and immediately asked if he could borrow the guitar and play something with us. Django couldn't play the standard type with an ordinary neck because of the damage his left hand had suffered in a caravan fire years before and he had to have a wider fretboard to play on. He sat in with us and it must have been one of the first occasions when he used an amplified guitar.

I played bass at the side of him and watched the way he played – the most remarkable guitarist in the world at that time. He had just his thumb and two fingers that he could use on his left hand and he played all his runs with those. But whenever he wanted to play an emphatic chord he would hoist across the fretboard his other two fingers, bent double and normally unusable, and then slash his right hand down on the strings with tremendous rhythmic force. It was an amazing spectacle. I remember we played a popular song of the time called 'La Mer'. It had been doing the rounds in London so I knew it well, and we played a few other things that all of us were familar with. He drove the group along with his unstoppable rhythm and played dazzling, intricate solos. Watching Django perform was an absolute revelation and being there and playing with him was something unforgettable.

A few days later there was another surprise. I had the chance to record with Django and Stéphane and the records we made are now quite famous. At the time, I was not aware of the whole background to what happened or how the sessions came about but it has since been written about a lot, for example by Charles Delaunay in his biography of Django, and in Geoffrey Smith's book on Grappelli.

The reason Django was in London was to meet up with Stéphane again. It was their first meeting since the war had begun six years before and, with peace now re-established in Europe after all the years of turmoil, it must have been a very emotional reunion for both of them. They were thinking about the possibility of reforming the Quintet of the Hot Club of France and doing some broadcasts in Britain. Django had actually kept the group going in France throughout the war with an almost completely different personnel but since the partnership of Grappelli and Reinhardt had been the really distinctive thing about the pre-war quintet, putting that together again would certainly have been a historic development. Django travelled from Paris to London on January 26th 1946, accompanied by his wife Naguine and his little son Babik. Grappelli had booked them all into the Athenaeum, which was where he lived, in a comfortable flat overlooking Green Park. They arrived there during the evening and waited for Grappelli who was working, as usual, at Hatchett's. Delaunay tells in his book what happened after that:

> As soon as work was over Stéphane made his appearance, accompanied by two of his sidemen... After embracings and reminiscences, Django, eager to hear his old colleague play again, learned that he had left his violin behind. One of the musicians left in haste to fetch an instrument, and shortly afterwards, in an atmosphere rich in nostalgic memories, Stéphane hesitatingly played the first few bars of the 'Marseillaise', and Django in turn, took up the tune. Without a moment's thought it was the national anthem, solemn and impassioned, that they had chosen to play. In a foreign country these two reprobates had given vent to the kind of patriotic gesture one would never have thought them capable of! And they spent the rest of the night playing

> together, improvising on tunes they had known so well ten years
> previously, or new songs, or melodies Django had composed dur-
> ing the war... They were still swinging when dawn broke over
> Green Park...

I wasn't there that night, but I took part in the recording
sessions that had been set up for the two of them a few days
later. I think Stéphane must have told Django, probably on
the night of January 26th, about the planned sessions and
the musicians he wanted to use on them, and Django must
have decided to come along to the Caribbean Club a day or
so later to hear me and see whether I measured up. A complication was that Django and Stéphane were contracted to
different recording companies at the time and that is probably why there were two sessions, one for HMV on January
31st at the Abbey Road studios in St. Johns Wood in north
west London and then another the following day for Decca
at their West Hampstead studios.

The idea at the sessions was partly, as Delaunay says in his
book, 'to recreate the atmosphere and the music of that
memorable night' of January 26-27th. Django was always
the complete bohemian, very unpredictable and impulsive.
His gypsy temperament would come out in all sorts of ways.
So the sessions had to be pretty businesslike to get the
music safely recorded while he was still in the mood. Apart
from Reinhardt, Grappelli and me, there were two British
guitarists, Jack Llewellyn and Alan Hodgkiss. So the set-up
of violin, three guitars and bass was exactly like the old pre-
war Hot Club quintet. I had to concentrate hard at those
sessions, because we had no rehearsal beforehand.
Everything was done there and then in the studio after we
had quickly worked out how we were going to play each
number. But it was exciting because I hadn't played in that
setting before, with the three guitars and violin.

Django and Stéphane talked to each other in French,
because Django had very little English, and we worked out
the arrangements on the spot. Of course, we recreated the

jazz version of 'The Marseillaise' that the two of them had improvised a few nights before. There was some apprehension about how that particular recording would be received. Some people probably thought it was very irreverent to be jazzing up the national anthem and, perhaps as a precaution, when it was released on record it was renamed 'Echoes of France'. Even so, it apparently displeased French officialdom and Stéphane later claimed that the master of that record was destroyed. Of course, playing 'The Marseillaise' was really a very emotional thing for them. They played it their way, expressing just what they felt at the time.

On 'Belleville' I had to do a modulation on my own, just the bass, and on several numbers I used my bow either for brief solo breaks (on 'Coquette', 'Lisa' and 'Belleville') or backing the other instruments (on 'Embraceable You'). The slow, bowed introduction with the violin on 'Echoes of France' was my idea. In fact, the way I played bass was very different from what Django was used to. I thought that the bass on the old Hot Club Quintet records was sometimes a bit stilted. Louis Vola, Django's bassist then, had a forceful, punchy style – a poom, poom, poom sound. But I liked something that flowed better with a relaxed, subtle swing. And Django hadn't worked before with jazz bassists who bowed, so that was also something new for him.

He was such a strange character. He always did things his way. Even when Stéphane would talk to him very seriously he would have his own idea about whatever they were talking about and always express matters in his different way. I suppose he had grown up doing things in a free and easy manner and it was natural to him. In their music, Django was always the dominant one. The whole thing revolved around him.

While he was in London, he came to visit Gertrude and me at home. He sat in a chair with Sandy, our baby daughter, on his knee and I took a photo of him with the

miniature camera I had at the time. Gertrude speaks good
French and chatted with him: he was going to the United
States and there was a plan, he told us, to make a film about
his life. He thought that the French would not have been
interested in anything like that – the gypsy caravan life –
but the Americans, with their Wild West history and wide
open spaces would find him and his background more hero-
ic. He had very romantic ideas about America.

Even though his English was so limited, I could talk with
him a bit. Throughout the time he was in London, he lived
on one of the upper floors in a hotel and down below there
was a club where I played one night. I went up in the lift
with Django and he told me then about his planned working visit to the States. He was very excited about it because
he was going to play with Duke Ellington. He said, 'Why
don't you come, too? Come to America with me.' But by
that time I had already decided that I didn't want to move
to the United States. Django did go to America and played
with Ellington. But his visit was not a success. He was very
disappointed by the reactions he got, which were warm but
not ecstatic. He thought he was a huge star – which he was
in musical terms – and that he should have been treated as
such, but musical styles were beginning to change by that
time and a lot of new things were happening in jazz, which
he hadn't quite picked up on. Going over there gave him a
big shock and he soon went back to France.

Years later, Gertrude and I were travelling through France
and we stopped in Paris and looked Django up. That was
early in 1951 and by then he was unwell and his career had
been in the doldrums. But, just at that time, things seemed
to be looking up for him again. He had a regular job at the
Club Saint-Germain where he was the star attraction, playing with a group of musicians much younger than himself.
He was living at a hotel just across the street with Naguine
and Babik, so that ensured that he was always on time for

the first set. In fact, when he wasn't working, he spent most of his time in bed in the hotel. He would get up to go to play and then go back to bed once he had finished the gig. We visited him at the hotel and Gertrude talked to him in French while he was sitting up in bed. He announced he was going to have another baby. Naguine, who was a very large lady, was there beside him and she just smiled when he said that. He talked about his little house on the banks of the Seine, near Fontainebleau, and also told Gertrude that he was very worried about sending his children to school. He could not read and write and perhaps he was afraid that their knowledge would leave him behind, or separate them from him.

We never saw him again and two years later he died. For me, having had the chance to make music with him a few years before had been a priceless experience. I felt I had been in very illustrious company.

I worked regularly at the Caribbean Club until the autumn of 1947. Although I loved being there and thought the atmosphere of the place was marvellous, I was never a great clubgoer. I remember one of the first places I went to in London was a club in Wardour Street where I was surprised to see a very young, absolutely gorgeous, tall blonde girl playing the saxophone. She was Kathy Stobart and I was astonished to hear how well she could play. Later, of course, she became a major player on the British jazz scene. That club was one place I would go to to sit in and have a little play.

At weekends, there were often gigs during the day and in the early 1940s I played regularly at Carlo Krahmer's Sunday afternoon sessions at the Feldman Club in Oxford Street. It's still there but now it's the 100 Club. The Feldman brothers would be on hand: Monty on accordion, Robert on clarinet, and amazing little Victor, who played drums. At some point Carlo would leave his drumkit to go for a break and Victor would come on and do his thing. He was a phenomenon, a child prodigy. When I played with him he was about nine, very tiny and his feet couldn't reach the drum pedals but he could already play the basics and Carlo gave him drum tuition. Later he became a brilliant pianist, vibraphonist and percussionist with an international reputation. After he moved to the States he worked and recorded with the bands of Woody Herman, Cannonball Adderley and Miles Davis and with his own groups.

During the week I always had a regular gig somewhere or other and over the years I kept up the pattern of weekend work too. But once I started a family with Gertrude and settled in the house in Notting Hill I generally wanted to get home after whatever job I was doing, spend time with the family and practise my instrument to keep on improving as a musician. When I was at the Caribbean Club, which was a day club, I didn't play any night clubs as well.

Strange as it may seem, I never even went to the Nest which was one of the most famous black clubs in London in the mid-1940s, a real meeting place. There was the Bag O'Nails too, and Jig's Club in Wardour Street. A kind of community of black musicians, especially West Indians, centred on those clubs. But most of the places involved a lot of drinking and dope-taking and I never wanted to get involved with that. I always kept away from places where it would be easy to be tempted, because I saw a lot of lives being damaged. In those days I didn't even drink. I only started to drink a bit, years later, when I worked with Joe Harriott at the Marquee. With Joe, the musicians would go to the pub between sets or afterwards and I liked a glass of beer. But in the post-war years I kept away from everything, because you could see how some people destroyed themselves with drink or drugs and wasted their talents completely.

Apart from that, I was always a keen sportsman and wanted to keep myself fit. There is no way you can do that if you are doping yourself up. Years before, when I was still in Jamaica, my father built a tennis court on the lawn of our house, so that's where the interest in tennis started and I never lost it. When I left Jamaica my mother gave me her tennis racket and I began playing here, first in Glasgow at the university and then in London. I became a member of Camden Hill Tennis Club in 1953, played in a lot of competitions and won a cup for the club. Now I'm an honorary member. So I've kept that up through the years.

The drug problem on the jazz scene gradually became much worse after the war. The situation changed as modern jazz came along in the late 1940s. In the early years, when I was with Johnny Claes, it was mainly just pot – marijuana – that musicians smoked. They would all get together to use the stuff and unless you did that you were not in the group and were not accepted. You would be invited to parties where dope was taken and if you wanted above everything to be part of a particular set there was a certain pressure. Either you did what they did or the party invitations stopped. But I figured I would get my pleasure in other ways, by playing in some group worth playing in which got its satisfaction from music, rather than from that other stuff. The drug problem became very serious when heroin took over from pot in the late forties, through the beginning of the fifties. It reached a kind of peak with the Tubby Hayes set. A lot of them were involved in one way or another and while they were alive they played fantastically. But some didn't live long.

At the end of the 1940s, new ideas about rhythm and harmony in jazz were coming to London from American records by Charlie Parker, Dizzy Gillespie and Thelonious Monk. A group of musicians who played at a basement in Windmill Street, eventually known as the Club Eleven, were the ones who first absorbed these ideas and developed them here. Tommy Pollard and trumpeter-pianist Denis Rose were key figures in that circle. Just before the Club Eleven started, Denis had been one of the musicians who sometimes sat in with our trio at the Caribbean Club. He was a very withdrawn character and had a most unusual embouchure as a trumpeter. He would point his trumpet down at the floor and seem to hang over it, almost blowing over the top. He didn't have a strong sound and later he concentrated mainly on playing piano, but he had very advanced ideas musically. He understood the new modern jazz idiom quickly and helped other musicians to learn the harmonies, chord formations, rhythms and so on.

Tommy Pollard understood all that too and developed a fine modern piano style, but both of them were terribly affected by drugs. I saw that with Denis at the Caribbean Club and it made me keep well away from him. When the modern jazz ideas came from America, the musicians who were attracted to them all wanted to sound like Parker, or as good as he did. Whatever instrument they played, they wanted to be Charlie Parkers and, of course, everyone knew Parker took heroin. So some of them thought, 'That's how he does it. I'll try that too,' even though he warned everyone that they should keep off that stuff.

Apart from Denis Rose (and Bertie King and Django), some other excellent musicians sat in or depped at the Caribbean Club. For example, Lauderic left for a time and Frank Deniz took his place. And other guitarists, especially Pete Chilver or Dave Goldberg, would come in sometimes to join us. Pete was a lovely player. In fact I loved his playing best of all, apart from Lauderic's. He was a very shy lad, withdrawn and quiet. In February 1947 I had a one-off job in Sheffield with a Canadian pianist named Art Thompson. Pete Chilver was booked for it too and I arranged to drive there taking him with me. I had a Vauxhall 10, which I had bought about eight months before.

In those days, with petrol rationing, you had to carry whatever petrol you needed in huge containers on a roof rack. So we set off, loaded with gallons of petrol up on top, Pete's guitar and my bass inside, and all the amplification equipment and the luggage. It was a really harrowing journey because that winter was terrible. It was the worst for years. The roads were like glass with black ice and it was blowing a blizzard. On the way back from the gig we got to a point where the road was straight and glistening with ice and a bus was coming in the opposite direction. I couldn't steer away without skidding because of the weight in the car and the bus came closer and closer and we were drifting across its track. Just as the back end of the car passed the bus it touched and the car spun right round on the ice. It slithered over to the side of the road and came to rest with the back wheels hanging over a drop of about thirty feet. Fortunately, in those days cars had starting handles. So we had to put the car in gear and slowly crank it out, winding it back over the edge of the drop and on to the road.

Pete Chilver was one of many guitarists who followed Lauderic's lead in the late forties and picked up on modern jazz harmonies and rhythmic and melodic ideas. But players of every instrument, if they were ambitious, were trying to learn about the new sounds. You had to do it from records, because there was no other way. Unless you could actually be in the clubs in New York or wherever, absorbing the atmosphere at first hand, you had to listen to records that came over here and learn from them, working out what was going on. That was obviously not as informative a method as hearing Parker and Gillespie and the other bebop pioneers in person, so some British musicians such as Ronnie Scott and Johnny Dankworth went to New York around 1947 to hear the new music at first hand and bring the ideas and some of the atmosphere back with them.

The advent of bebop certainly made a huge difference. It was a massive onslaught on one's own musical background and at the beginning it was very hard to understand. The harmonies sounded odd, the rhythms were strange and the melodic lines the soloists played sometimes seemed bizarre. It was very difficult and I wasn't sure whether I would like it or not. It was completely different from what we were used to and it took time to appreciate what was going on. Years later you think, 'Why did I ever find that difficult? It seems perfectly OK now. Why was there a problem to start with? Why couldn't it be accepted straight away? Why did it take years before everyone could say it's great, it's lovely?' I had to adjust my ideas gradually to appreciate bebop and, because of that, I could perhaps understand the reaction of musicians in London more than a decade later when we introduced free form music in the repertoire of the Joe Harriott Quintet. They had never heard anything like it before and it was completely alien to what they had been hearing.

If you are going to be able to play any music you have to be able to *feel* it. It's not a question of one note following another, so that you read it off in some mechanical way. You have to feel what you are playing if it is going to have meaning. With bebop and modern jazz, the people who developed it in New York worked it out gradually and grew with it. But here in London we were just getting the finished product. So it was necessary to become familiar with the sounds, to get used to them, and then they gradually became natural to us. Sound evokes feelings and if you aren't familiar with the sounds you haven't experienced the feelings that go with them. When you have heard enough, you start to expect certain things to happen in the music and when they do, it feels right. Until you've got to that stage it is difficult to accept, appreciate and understand new musical ideas.

When I first heard Charlie Parker's alto saxophone I was astonished at the way he weaved around chord sequences that we had been using in quite different ways – 'Cherokee', for example. He created a different sort of melody from the same chord structure, and then altered the chords, extending the harmonies. When you originally heard that chord structure, before bebop came along, it naturally suggested certain melodic lines to you. But when Parker played it, the melodic lines were nothing like what you expected. You thought, 'How did he do that? What is he doing?' The melodic approach was completely different and the harmonies were altered, even though you could hear something familiar there.

Listening to Clifford Brown, the trumpeter, on record a few years later helped me a lot. I could appreciate his approach and his musicianship shone through. But that is a very personal thing. Certain musicians affect you more than others because they do things in a way that is closer to the way you do them and the way you feel. What affects one person may not affect another.

Gradually I adapted my bass playing to modern jazz. It wasn't a matter of following new theories but of learning to hear new harmonic and melodic possibilities, becoming familiar with them. You begin to appreciate all the possible notes in any given situation. You can study chords and learn it that way, but, in my case at least, it was a matter of hearing enough of the music and having enough of a musical background to appreciate what was going on. You hear certain progressions against a certain melody line and you begin to feel what is right to play.

Perhaps I can put it this way. When Django, Stéphane and the rest of us recorded 'Echoes of France', you could say there was no familiar chord sequence that we could use for jazz improvisation, because we just took a few lines of the French national anthem as a starting point. But when I thought of that tune it immediately suggested a chord sequence and a bass line. If I hear a melody I automatically hear a chord sequence that can go with it and then I can choose bass notes from the harmonies I hear in my head. When bebop came in, it wasn't so simple. You had to learn to hear new harmonies, more advanced chords, different inversions. It wasn't a matter of unlearning anything but of extending the understanding of harmony that you already had. You need to carry all your knowledge with you but know where to place it. Different things relate to different times and circumstances. In the end, though, the main thing was still to be able to hear those harmonies in your head automatically and feel intuitively how to use them as imaginatively as possible to enrich a melodic line and to make the music satisfying.

The ideas coming into modern jazz were challenging. They made it a more complex, serious music. But I always appreciated the fun side of jazz too – the sort of jivey, joke-filled music that Louis Jordan and Slim Gaillard produced. Eventually Lauderic, Dick Katz and I found a way to combine the two things: doing our best to make adventurous music, on the one hand, and making sure the audience was entertained and had plenty of fun, on the other. Strangely enough, it came about indirectly through Stéphane Grappelli.

Grappelli had the job of providing music for a film sometime towards the end of 1946. It was just a short feature that, as Geoffrey Smith says in his book about Stéphane, 'gives a vintage view both of a Grappelli band at work and the musical climate of the time.' Shearing was the pianist, Dave Goldberg was on guitar, I played bass and the group was completed by a drummer named Ray Ellington. On the film, we play several of Stéphane's compositions, including his theme song 'The Stéphane Blues'; 'Piccadilly Stomp' which he had written before the war; 'Wendy', a pretty song dedicated to George's daughter; and 'Eveline', dedicated to his own. Ray Ellington does a bop-style vocal on 'Sweet Georgia Brown' and splits a chorus with my bowed and hummed solo bass. After we have finished playing, the announcer says, 'I hope drummer Ray Ellington feels better now, having got all that rebop off his chest.' In those days, rebop was another name for modern jazz or bebop.

On screen, we are all dressed immaculately in dinner-jackets, as though playing in a high class club and we beam at the camera and look as though we are reacting warmly to each other. All that smiling wasn't just show, because the session was a lot of fun and went well. The announcer says at the end of the film, 'Well, these boys certainly seem to enjoy themselves' and we did.

That was the first time I had played with Ray Ellington and I realised that he was an excellent drummer and a great personality. It was that combination which gave a special lift to those filmed performances. He had a very good voice and I realised he was extremely versatile. After all, as Geoffrey Smith says, in the film we played 'some rebop, some swing, some elegant sentiment, something for every sophisticated taste, impeccably done.'

It occurred to me that Ray was just the right person to join with our trio at the Caribbean Club and make a kind of show group. He had the personality that was required. He could bring in some of the humour that I liked in jazz, and his excellent musical skills matched the kind of sophistication we had tried to develop with the trio. He had been featured as a star attraction in Harry Roy's orchestra on drums and with a comedy routine that went down well with audiences. He really had the gift of presentation that could make a show. And he was very receptive to the sophisticated new ideas in jazz, had led small groups of his own and was no stranger to broadcasting. So he already had something of a name nationally. I thought all that made an impressive combination.

During the lunch interval in the day's filming, I went for a drink with him in the local pub and put the proposition to him. He said he thought it could be a good idea. Of course, Lauderic and Dick didn't know anything about this so I had to take the idea back to them and see what they thought. It wouldn't just be a matter of adding a drummer to the trio, after all. With everything that Ray would bring, adding him would change things fundamentally.

I convinced them and eventually we did get together with Ray. But it was some time before the new group was ready to meet the public. The Caribbean Trio stayed as it was for a time, working in the club as before. Meanwhile we started rehearsing with Ray. A friend of his, a black American dance teacher and choreographer named Buddy Bradley, had a room above the club where he ran his dance studio and he allowed the four of us to use it for rehearsals. Buddy knew how to put together a stage show so that it would go over well with the audience. So he would suggest ideas about presentation and we worked out routines and new pieces to play.

It must have been during that period that Stéphane's quintet, the group that had played in the film, went into the Decca recording studios. I don't remember the circumstances now, but I still have copies of some of the records we made. There were four titles, 'Yellow House Stomp', 'Red-O-Ray', 'Channel Crossing' and 'In the Mood', recorded on April 25th 1947. So I was getting used to working with Ray Ellington in various contexts.

The rehearsals went on and eventually the question of a name for the group came up. I think it was Buddy Bradley who suggested we should call ourselves the Ray Ellington Quartet. The idea was that Ray would be the one who was up front. He would obviously tend to be the centre of the show, having had plenty of public exposure with Harry Roy and elsewhere and having been on BBC 'Jazz Club' as a known jazzman. His name carried much more weight for publicity purposes than that of the Caribbean Trio. Calling the group the Caribbean Quartet – as we did on the broadcast with Bertie King – would not have had as much pulling power. So we went along with the idea. The Ray Ellington Quartet came into being, quietly, without any fuss, in the room above the Caribbean Club. And eventually, after much rehearsing and planning and putting together all our best ideas, we were ready to go out and conquer the world. I certainly thought that with Ray on board and with what we had already achieved with the trio we had a good formula. But, of course, none of us had any idea that our little group was going to hit the jackpot and become one of the most popular small bands in the country.

5.

Ellingtonians

Ray Ellington was an imposing chap. He was dapper, well-dressed and well-groomed with his neat, trimmed moustache and he carried himself magnificently. He was tall for the time – six feet two – but you didn't particularly notice his height because he was broad-shouldered and well proportioned. And he always kept his fine body in good trim. Ray had real presence on stage with his smile and sense of humour, and with all of that going for him, of course he was a much admired character as far as the ladies were concerned.

He also had an unusual background which, Spike Milligan joked, 'had him screwed up for a lifetime'. His father was a black American comedian from St. Louis, Missouri, and his mother, who was Jewish, had been born in Russia. But Ray had grown up in the hardly exotic surroundings of Lambeth in south London and, according to Val Wilmer who recently discovered his birth certificate, his original name (like his father's) was plain Harry Brown. When Duke Ellington visited London in 1933, young Harry had just started playing drums and went to hear him, being totally knocked out by the experience. After that he changed his surname to that of his new idol and set out on his musical career with the Duke's full-blooded jazz, rather than the sweet dance music of the day, as his model. He soon became a real show-man as well as a highly skilled drummer. So in 1947 this was the new leader of our group, parachuted in, so to speak, to a band that had already been in existence for three years.

Much of the music of the Ray Ellington Quartet was in place, in a way, when the group was formed. Dick, Lauderic and I had been working together for so long that we knew how to interact musically and had plenty of material and our own style. But I realised that if we were going to break out and make a mark in wider entertainment circles we needed to build a show, and mix humour in with the musical sophistication. I could see how it could work and that was why I had approached Ray. He had the extra ele-ment the group needed.

We decided on a policy of putting children's nursery rhymes into a sort of sophisticated jazz context. The idea was to try to be as interesting as possible musically and put a lot of fun into the music and give it a broad appeal. So we did a jazz version of 'The Three Bears' and it went down well with audiences. They loved it. In January 1948 we recorded the song and it became the group's first big hit. Later we followed that with Ray's version of 'Little Bo(p) Peep' which featured his bebop vocalese style and some sur-real lyrics, and 'Old King Cole' done in a similar way, with a hip vocal line that Ray and I shared, and each member of the group featured in turn in brief solos in the arrangement.

We used all kinds of ideas, trying to keep plenty of variety, but always with a solid musical content. Some vocal num-bers featuring Ray were influenced by what the Nat Cole Trio had been recording around that time. On the quartet's 1949 recording of 'You Can't Judge a Book by the Cover', Ray's singing style sounds a lot like Nat Cole's, and we used some of Nat's material, recording his song 'It Is Better To Be By Yourself' at our second recording session in February 1948. But we never stayed in one place musically for long. We did versions of Louis Jordan hits such as 'Beware' and 'Five Guys Named Mo' and there were crazy novelty numbers like 'The Maharajah of Magador' and the anarchic 'I Didn't Know the Gun Was Loaded' on which I brought out my violin and played barn-dance fiddle. We usually found space for jazz solos and always for plenty of jazz feeling amongst the mayhem. And we mixed in purely instrumental numbers that showed off the kind of intricate, ever-shifting arrangements and neat, driving solos we had perfected in the Caribbean Trio. Tracks such as 'Dream for Percussion' and 'Dick's Boogie' display that side of what the quartet did on record.

Someone, maybe a producer, came up with the idea that each of us in the group should write a composition to record. So 'Dick's Boogie' was Dick Katz's contribution and it shows off his dazzling piano technique. Ray wrote the complex 'Dream for Percussion' and I did a 'Dream for Bass' – the only piece of music I've ever written – which features bowed bass at two different tempos. Lauderic produced a fast and furious bebop piece with vaguely oriental overtones. We worked on it as a group and came up with what would now be thought a very politically incorrect bit of vocal fooling to frame the guitar theme. Ray sang scat in what amounted to his version of 'Chinese' and when we put everything together the number was titled 'China Bop'.

The public liked the musical mix and we soon found we were attracting big audiences and the records sold well. At that time, just a few years after the war, people had a great need for something to lift their spirits and what we were doing suited the times. To have light comedy in music was like the safety valve letting off steam, because things had been so desperately grim through the war years. And we made sure the group and its presentation were as good as we could make them from the beginning, before we went out to meet the public.

Ray and I were the two scatty ones. Scatty but also serious-minded, I hope, when we needed to be. Often, when Ray did a humorous vocal I would take on the role of heckler or encourager, throwing in some crazy patter behind him. Lauderic, being always a very serious guy, found it hard to adapt to some things we were putting in the music, but he did his best and can be heard contributing a gruff vocal chorus on the recording of 'The Maharajah of Magador'. But to be funny wasn't really Lauderic's bag at all. It was very difficult for him and he was shy about it. Dick, by contrast, was easy about the whole thing. He was an unusual chap. For a German in those days to play jazz as well as he did was absolutely exceptional and Germans are usually pretty serious people. But underneath the surface he liked the mad, funny elements in the music. It was new and different and he had the talent to bring it off.

The quartet's records give a good representation of what we did in live performance. Nowadays, of course, a jazz group might play a particular piece in concert or in a club in a much longer version than they would on record. There might be much more time given over to the solos in a live performance. But in the 1940s everything about performance was governed by the three minutes that 78 rpm records could run for. That regime was instilled into us because as musicians you always had to be able to produce a three minute performance to order in the recording studio. The freedom to stretch out came only much later when long play and extended play records came in. So when I was with Ray Ellington it would never occur to us to play a piece that would not fit the three minute frame, even if we were playing in a club or a concert. In any case, the arrangements were in our heads and that fixed how much improvisation there was going to be in any piece and where it would come.

From the beginning we were able to get radio broadcasts and the quartet recorded regularly every few months. Then the records started coming out and people everywhere began to be aware of the group. *Melody Maker*, the main popular music paper, gave us good publicity. Edgar Jackson, who reviewed jazz records for the magazine and had been its first editor, was a great supporter. But we had a serious setback the first time we went out on the road.

One of our very first engagements was at a restaurant in Edinburgh. At that time Dick Katz rode a motorbike, an Ariel Square Four, and the night before we were due to set off for Scotland something was wrong with it. He worked on it through the night but the problem was still there in the morning and he decided to call at Birmingham on the way to have some emergency repairs done by the makers. He set off and I drove behind him in my car. But he was completely tired out from working on the bike all night and at some point on the way to Birmingham he started to fall asleep while riding along. Following him, I saw it happen and couldn't do anything to stop it. As he nodded off he drifted in to the path of a car coming in the opposite direction and caught its tail end with his wheel. He was thrown off and badly injured. So he ended up in hospital and we had to do the Edinburgh gig with a replacement pianist. Of course, it didn't work. Dick was irreplaceable. But the show had to go on and we did about three weeks without him. Certainly he was lucky to survive.

Concerts at the London Palladium also helped spread the word about our music. The Palladium had a long-running Sunday 'Swing Sessions' series featuring Ted Heath's Orchestra and Ted would invite guest artistes. Our first major appearance was at a Swing Session on December 7th

1947. *Checkers*, a new magazine for the British black community, carried a feature about the quartet a few months later and wrote about the Palladium concert:

> From the opening bars of the Ellington show.... the audience swayed in their seats and after each number shrieked, whistled, stamped and shouted for more and still more. A perspiring Ray gasped his appreciation, the Heath boys put aside their instruments and joined with the audience in acknowledgement of four brilliant musicians. For this phenomenal new outfit had presented a superb show and a 'New Look' in modern music. A 'be-boppish' offering which avoided the hackneyed riffs and stilted cliches which are the pitfall of so many Dizzy Gillespie imitators.

At another Swing Session, in October 1948, Ella Fitzgerald sang. That was during her first trip away from the United States and she was billed in London as a variety artiste to avoid the Musicians Union ban, then in force, on American musicians appearing in Britain. The great Ray Brown, married to her at that time, led the accompanying trio. Ray hadn't brought his own bass with him to London. His practice then was to find a good instrument wherever he was going to play and use that. On this occasion he had to choose between my bass or the one belonging to Charlie Short, the bassist in Heath's band. He chose mine and played it in his own superb style throughout his part of the concert. That's something you don't forget!

I kept in touch with him after that and years later when he was in London again to do a concert at Hammersmith we played informally together. He was carrying a book of duets around with him on his travels. They were adaptations by Fred Zimmerman from Bach, Mozart, Haydn, Handel and other composers. The idea came up that we might play them together on our basses so I took my instrument to his hotel in Paddington and afterwards he gave me the book we had played from and inscribed it 'to my man, Coleridge'. He was a wonderful bassist and it was a terrible shock for me when he died recently, because he was playing superbly right up to the end of his life.

Apart from stage shows like the Swing Sessions, we played mostly dance halls and soon found we were working all the time, fifty weeks of the year. Harold Davison of Bernard Delfont's office, who was our agent, made sure we kept busy. The *Checkers* article summed it up: 'The Quartet travelled from town to town [throughout 1948], covering thousands of miles by road and rail. From every quarter of the British Isles came the same story – box office records broken again and again, tickets sold out weeks before the events were due to take place. For Ray and the boys huge stacks of 'fan' mail awaited their return to London.'

We would be booked as the intermission cabaret at a dance hall in some town or other. The resident band would play its first set for dancing and during its break we would do our show. The dancers would crowd round, standing packed close in front of the bandstand to see our act and from the stage we could look across the dark hall and see some of their faces and judge how the music was going over.

We made very good money. The group was always well paid and we stayed in good hotels, which was a difference from the usual kinds of digs you encounter as a musician on tour – the sort of places I eventually became very familiar with over the years. The quartet usually played a week or so in one place and then moved on. And that was my first experience of being on the road all the time. With Claes and Winstone it had just been occasional work entertaining the troops that took us out of London and the furthest afield we went was probably Bournemouth or Brighton.

By the time I was with Ray Ellington I always travelled in my own car and, with all the gear I had, that was an absolute necessity. Dick soon gave up riding his motorbike and he and Ray travelled mostly by train. Ray would take taxis to and from the station and move his drums around that way. Much later, Phil Seamen always used to travel the same way – taxis and trains – when he was our drummer in Joe Harriott's quintet.

I enjoyed driving on my own, finding my way to wherever the quartet was booked to play. Being on the road as a touring musician was something new for me and it was exciting. The roads were not as good as they are now but there was much less traffic on them. They were narrower but cars were smaller and as a musician you must be prepared to go anywhere, learn to get around and put up with whatever discomforts come your way.

You certainly get a sense of freedom, but unless you're booked into a first class hotel you never know what sort of conditions you are going to find, what the digs are going to be like, and if you are going somewhere to play for a week it is certainly important to have a nice place to stay. If you are only doing one-nighters then at least it's only for that night if the digs turn out to be lousy.

Of course, I ran into discrimination, and not just in finding digs. But the way I look at it is that people who discriminate are not the sort of people I should bother myself about. If they cannot see that a black person can be a good, useful citizen and can do a good job, as well as he can, then their heads are wrong and I don't think I should worry about such people. You have to know that discrimination happens and that you are going to come up against it. But you have to think beyond it and realise it's not something worth making yourself sick about. Have confidence in your own abilities and your own worth.

It can be different in some ways with a predominantly black band. At least you have other sufferers with you! You're not on your own and there's someone to share the bad things with, which makes it a little bit easier. But, on the other hand, there was a lot of competition for jobs in music at the time when the Ray Ellington Quartet was getting so much work. People would look at you if you were successful and you were doing well and some of them would be thinking, 'Why couldn't I be in his job?' I suppose some musicians looked at things that way and if you are not exactly like them in one way or another they might feel put upon that it's you and not them, thinking that they should be getting the work and the success. Being on the receiving end of attitudes like that isn't pleasant when it happens to you but you've got to understand that it does, and put it behind you. I'm sure there was some of that antagonism to the quartet. But it didn't affect us a lot. We knew our worth. We knew we were doing a good job and that we earned every penny we got.

It was a good existence, on the whole, being 'Ellingtonians' and we had the chance to meet and work alongside a lot of fine musicians on the various circuits we travelled. During the first year of the band's existence we even had the chance to record with an Ellingtonian in the other sense, one of Duke Ellington's sidemen. That was Ray Nance, Duke's star trumpeter, violinist and vocalist. He came to England with Duke and the singer Kay Davis in June 1948 and they appeared at the London Palladium and went on tour. In the same way as Ella and Ray Brown a few months later, they avoided the British union ban on American musicians by presenting themselves as a variety act.

Carlo Krahmer, who had started his own Esquire record label just a few months earlier, set up a recording session on July 1st for Ray Nance and hired the Ray Ellington Quartet to back him. Because the quartet was contracted to Parlophone we couldn't use our own names on the records, so they were issued, accurately if misleadingly, as by 'Ray Nance and the Ellingtonians' and we each had a pseudonym. I was 'George Goodwin'.

Carlo lived, as he had for years, in Bloomsbury in central London in a big flat in Bedford Court Mansions with his wife Greta and he had his recording studio there in the basement. There were endless rows of records around the walls, the recording equipment was all at one end of the room and he had a big Voigt speaker, which at the time was the best you could get. Carlo's flat was a popular meeting place for musicians. I already knew the place because I used to go there occasionally since the time he and I had first known each other working with Johnny Claes. He had excellent sound equipment and used to import Duke Ellington records from the States. I loved go to Carlo's and hear the sound of Jimmy Blanton's bass on his audio set-up.

We all got on well at the session with Ray Nance. It was an experience to play with him and he was easy to work with. There was no advance planning. We met at the studio and he suggested things we might play including a version of the lovely ballad 'Moon Mist' which features his violin, as on the classic Duke Ellington recording of a few years before. 'Blues for Duke' starts with slow bowed bass. Nance starts on trumpet and finishes, after Dick's solo, on violin – the same pattern he uses on 'Sometimes I'm Happy'. 'I Can't Give You Anything but Love' has some of his inimitable singing. Making those records was fun and special and I think they still sound good today.

The quartet's records, broadcasts and appearances worked together to build our public following and as this happened the pressure to travel at home and abroad gradually became more and more intense. In the spring of 1949, soon after the heavy touring had started, Lauderic suddenly left. We went up to Thirsk in Yorkshire and he left the group there. He always hated being out of London and the slightest thing could upset him. He wasn't ill, as far as I remember. Probably it was mainly that he just felt too far away from where he wanted to be. That was always Lauderic's problem. He hated travelling. I built an amplifier that he and I could both plug into and we used it a lot, for example on the Ray Nance session and on a gig in Brighton, part of which was recorded. So, when we travelled, I would take this amplifier which served for both the bass and the guitar. All he needed to take was his guitar and he could go by train. But in the end none of that solved the problem. Just as he had done with Claes, he set off for home and left the band.

He was always very complex but also, by that time, he was getting disillusioned with all kinds of things. He had had high ambitions for his music and wanted it to be taken very seriously. He had been writing music from the time he was with Johnny Claes and eventually he wrote a major composition and entered and had it accepted for the prestigious Italia Prize. As far as I know, it didn't win but it was good enough to be accepted as an entry and the BBC had some kind of interest in the competition. But then a magazine printed a picture of Lauderic in a very happy mood wearing a rakish beret and generally looking not at all like the proper image of a serious musician, as some people might think. The BBC people saw the picture and from that time they dropped Lauderic and his music completely. Before that they were going to promote his composing but afterwards everything changed.

That had a terrible effect on him. He was a real original and had a lot to give, but he was very pessimistic about his prospects as a serious musician from then on. He felt rejected. The racial insults he had suffered at various times and the sense of not fitting the image – these things were all mixed up. Perhaps also he never really settled in to the sort of musical entertainment style that the quartet was trying to develop. It didn't suit his character.

After he left the quartet he did some acting, sang in vocal

groups and gradually drifted away from music. He worked with various small bands including some with Louis Stephenson who was a good alto saxophone player and Lauderic's life-long friend. In fact, Lauderic and I played together again for a brief period in the mid-1950s. But by the end of that decade he had given up the guitar altogether and I lost touch with him because I was into a completely different set of circumstances playing with Joe Harriott. After that, he got work as a driver, wrote some unpublished novels, took up yoga and gradually became more and more of a recluse, almost a hermit. He locked himself away and eventually he didn't see anybody and didn't want to. It was all a great loss as far as his musical talent was concerned and very sad. But, fortunately, on a lot of the Ray Ellington Quartet records you can still hear what a wonderful jazz improviser he was.

Lauderic's replacement was Laurie Deniz, the youngest of the three guitar-playing Deniz brothers. They came originally from Tiger Bay in Cardiff, their seaman father having been born in the Portuguese Cape Verde Islands. I knew all the family well and had worked with Frank, the eldest brother, in Eric Winstone's group and at the Caribbean Club. Laurie was technically a very good player with a fluent, melodic style, rhythmically very subtle. He was fourteen years younger than Lauderic, really the next generation, and had a completely different way of playing. He brought a fully formed modern jazz style of the kind that the young guitarists were using then, with a very even rhythm, fast fingering and a sort of cloudy tone. Lauderic's style was more personal because he had developed it through the transition from swing to bebop but Laurie suited the quartet well and I think he was much more into the fun side of the music than Lauderic had been.

I became fairly close to Laurie whereas the other two, Dick and Ray, tended to be together because they were the ones who travelled by train. Like me, Laurie had his own car and we often arranged to travel at more or less the same time in our vehicles to look out for each other and make sure each of us made the journey without problems. All four of us got on well but there wasn't a lot of social life amongst us. We spent a lot of time together but it was all business: rehearsing, doing the shows or travelling. When we would get to a hotel, Ray would usually find himself a girlfriend and so you wouldn't see much of him after that until it was time to work again. And I always travelled on my own in the car, so there wasn't any social life on the road. But, as I said, I loved the travelling, the freedom of the open road.

Before long we started touring abroad. The first trip was to Holland where the group had a residency in a night club in Amsterdam for three weeks and ended the stay with a performance at the famous Concertgebouw. We also did radio broadcasts from Hilversum. It all went well, we got good audiences and the Dutch musicians gave us a great welcome and I remember among them Ria Joy, a lovely young woman who sang in a Billie Holiday style.

We also went to Berlin in 1949. All the city seemed to be rubble. It was horrific. When I saw the devastation the wartime bombing had caused I thought, 'It'll take them fifty years to clear all this.' In fact I went back a few years later and the rubble had gone, but four years after the war had ended the place was still a complete wasteland. We travelled by train to Berlin and the organisers drove us from the station in a Volkswagen to a house that had belonged to Hermann Goering. It had somehow escaped the bombing and I remember a most beautiful grand piano there. That was where we stayed. We did a feature spot in a concert before a huge audience. People were starved of entertainment in those grim years and the reception was wonderful.

Tito Gobbi, the opera singer, was one of the stars in the show so I heard his lovely voice backed by an excellent German radio orchestra.

The most memorable foreign trip was to Sweden in 1950. We toured all round the country from city to city. They would put on entertainment in the parks and we would play there, often in the open air. We were always the star attraction so, unlike the time in Berlin, we had the concerts to ourselves. And they always attracted big audiences. Of course the distances were great. To get to each town took a long time and it would be a matter of arriving and setting up, maybe doing a rehearsal, getting the feel of the place and trying out the sound, and then playing the concert.

As always when we toured, I travelled on my own in my little Vauxhall 10-4. It was a nice, comfortable car – the first to have independent front wheel suspension, torsion bar suspension – and to make it more comfortable I used an inflated air-bed to sit on. So that was real armchair luxury which made travelling relatively easy. And a paraffin heater in the car kept me warm. It wasn't difficult to snooze off in those conditions so I would have to stop every so often to relax. The bass was inside the car on the front passenger seat, the amplifier was packed on the roof rack and I would drive for incredible distances like that.

The first memorable experience of the trip was arriving in Stockholm late at night. The ship from Britain came in to Gothenburg and once the car was unloaded I drove across the country from south to north. So it was dark by the time I reached the outskirts of Stockholm. The old town centre is surrounded by water and most of the city is built on islands. I drove over a bridge and saw a blaze of lights from all the buildings, with twinkling reflections of the bright illuminations in the water. What a contrast with London which always seemed dark, blacked out and miserable throughout the post-war austerity years! And, even more, what a contrast with the shattered Berlin I had seen a few months before!

Stockholm was a glorious sight and as I saw more of Sweden, I came to love the country: what it stood for and how the Swedes looked after their people – the social security, the sensible planning, the fine old people's homes, the excellent medical facilities and, above all, the cleanliness. People on the streets looked smart and well taken care of and even the messenger boys wore suits. In Stockholm the car needed repairs so I drove to an underground garage and before I had even got out of my seat a device had been fitted to the exhaust pipe to take any engine fumes out of the garage building. Then I saw the mechanics in white spotless uniforms, not at all greasy. The floor was clean too, and protective coverings were spread out to work on. The whole approach was to ensure cleanliness and it was very striking, coming from London at that time. I liked their socialist system and the way they tried to ensure social welfare for everyone. Later I began to learn Swedish because I thought seriously about moving there to live, but with family and career commitments that didn't turn out to be possible.

The tour started with concerts in Stockholm at the Stora Scenen (in Swedish, 'big scene'), a large platform stage in an amusement park used for all kinds of entertainments. At one corner of the platform was a very tall pole on the top of which acrobats did their acts, and the pole would bend and sway in the breeze as they climbed it. We had a big surprise at the first concert on the open-air stage. In front of it was a huge open space where people could stand and when we played on that warm summer evening the whole area was packed with people. A crowd of 20,000 had come to hear us. We had never known anything like it before. I looked out over the crowd from that platform and it was just an endless sea of heads. The show went fantastically well. There were acrobats and other people on the bill, but we were the only band and the crowd really loved the music. It was a wonderful experience.

The quartet played several nights at Stora Scenen and in the afternoons we would go there to rehearse on the platform stage. I think it was during the first afternoon that I was surprised to hear the distant sound of a baritone saxophone coming from somewhere below the stage. Someone was practising alone and the soft phrases that drifted up struck me as lovely and unlike anything I had heard before. Whoever was playing had a gorgeous tone and lyrical, gentle style. I could not see where the sound came from at first but then I noticed a small open-fronted, roofed-over area to the left of the stage. I went down to find out who was playing and discovered the solitary baritone player there. I told him I loved the sound of his saxophone and he introduced himself as Lars Gullin.

He was a young man in his early twenties and was not yet known at all outside Sweden. At the time he was working with Seymour Osterwall's dance orchestra and it would be the following year before he had the chance to record under his own name and with James Moody and Stan Getz. After that, his records gradually began to be heard widely around Europe and in America and he started winning international jazz polls in magazines such as *Down Beat*. His career took off and he became recognised as one of the finest baritone sax players in the world and a very talented jazz composer. In later years I always looked out for his records and bought many of them.

We didn't say much to each other at that first meeting, but I ran into Lars again nearly a decade later, in San Remo in 1959 when I was playing at a festival there with Joe Harriott. We had the chance to play together then. But by that time he was a very sick man. He had become a heroin addict and had ruined his health with drugs. We spent a lot of time talking and I wasn't surprised to find that he was intelligent, warm and gentle, just as his music suggested. He was subdued and didn't seem to have much vigour but his ill health had not noticeably affected his playing.

We walked along the glorious San Remo beach and talked about life and music, the delightful place where we were staying, and how good it was to be in each other's company. Swedish people are often reserved but when fellow musicians, wherever they come from, appreciate each other's work they tend to come out of their shell. He talked slowly but very forthrightly. We got on very well and I was fond of him as a person. He was just a thoroughly good man with no evil thoughts. It's such a tragedy that he did not have the chance to fulfil all his potential. Nowadays his music ought to be heard much more widely because it is beautiful and unique. He was a great musician, but he died in the mid-1970s when he was only in his forties.

Apart from Gullin, I didn't meet any of the young generation of Swedish musicians on that 1950 tour. Stora Scenen was on the edge of Skansen, the big grassy park where bands played in the summer months, and I would walk through there occasionally and listen to some of the music. People like alto sax player Arne Domnérus, clarinettist Putte Wickman and pianist Bengt Hallberg could often be heard. I still have an album of three 78 rpm records by Domnérus' 'Favourite Group' and 'Favourite Five'. They were the first records he made, in 1949, around the time when his appearance at the Paris Jazz Fair suddenly made a lot of people aware of the quality of Swedish modern jazz. They were newly released when I was in Stockholm with Ray Ellington and I must have bought them then – the first of many beautiful Swedish jazz records I gradually collected.

After the Stockholm concerts, we played in Gothenburg and then all over the country and I drove for miles in the Vauxhall. Fortunately the roads were generally very good. One evening we had a gig in the north of the country and then the next engagement was down south the following day. So that was a vast distance to drive and the gig in the south was scheduled for midday so there was no question of staying the night before setting off after the previous concert. I had to get in the car straight away and drive through the night. I would have breaks and a nap or two in the car. That's not enough to refresh you, of course, but it was all I could do and then I had to go on stage almost as soon as I arrived at the destination. That was the schedule: it was terrible but we had to do it.

So by the time the concert in the south had finished I was tired out, but then the plan was to get back to Stockholm immediately because we had a hotel booking. I didn't know how I was going to keep driving and not fall asleep at the wheel and have a crash. It was Sunday so almost all shops were closed but I found an apotek – a chemist – and the only things they could sell me to keep me awake were caffeine tablets. I kept taking them and they stopped me falling asleep until I was back in Stockholm. But after that I tasted coffee for months. I couldn't get rid of the taste whatever I ate or drank. It turned me off coffee for the rest of my life and I have never really drunk it since.

One beautiful place we visited was Östersund, in the mid-north of Sweden. I remember well how clean the air was. You could stand there and see for miles and everything in the distance was sharp and clear because the air had no impurities in it. Sweden made such an impression that I was determined to go back. I wanted to show Gertrude this lovely country and a decade later, in 1960, we had a holiday there together and visited many of the places I had been to with the quartet. On that occasion we spent time with Jimmy Woode, who had been Duke Ellington's bass player and had recently moved to Sweden with his father to live.

***

While I was travelling in Britain and abroad with Ray Ellington, Gertrude usually stayed at home to look after our daughter. Sandy was just two years old when the quartet came into existence so she was too young to travel much. I had to leave the family behind and spend a lot of time away. As a professional musician you must travel, you need to take your music around to keep people interested. It's part of the life. Obviously everything isn't always going to go smoothly but the important thing is to do the gig. The job is very important. If you're not good at it and you let the team down the whole thing suffers. If that happens you are not being good to your family either because if you are not successful you don't bring the money home. With Ray I was certainly bringing the money home and that helped us enormously. It meant Gertrude and Sandy could live a better life than they would have had otherwise. After all, many people had a very tough existence at that time with rationing and post-war shortages.

But there was an occasion when the family travelled with me. In the spring of 1951 the quartet was booked to play a nightclub in Milan. For once, Gertrude and I decided that we would make the trip together and take Sandy. Gertrude loves Italy and we were looking forward to the stay there. But, in fact, it turned out to be a disaster and the end of the line as far as my involvement with the band was concerned.

The quartet arranged to meet in Milan on Good Friday, March 23rd. Laurie Deniz set off from London in his car, and Gertrude, Sandy and I travelled in ours, but the journey was dreadful. The car was loaded with all our gear: several suitcases, my amplification system, the bass, the roofrack piled up with stuff. At some point we went over a big pothole and the car bottomed with a great bang. Eventually we were under way again but later, driving down a hill, I put my foot on the brake pedal and nothing happened. It was panic stations, and I had to use the handbrake and gears to slow down and avoid crashing into the curve at the foot of the hill. What had happened was that when the car bottomed the brake pipe split and I lost all the brake fluid without knowing. I managed to stop but we were very lucky to be alive. Then there was great difficulty getting the repairs done quickly so as to get to our destination in time and, to cap everything, just before we reached Milan the torsion bar broke.

Eventually we drove into the city but there was no sign of Ray and Dick at the agreed time and place and no way of contacting them. The plan, as usual, had been that they would make the journey by train. We waited for a long time without news. Eventually the phone rang in our room in the hotel where the quartet was booked to stay. Ray and Dick had reached Calais on the Channel ferry but not been able to get any further. Dick had never been naturalised as British and remained a German national. He had forgotten to get a visa, which he needed at that time, and the French officials would not let him through immigration control to take the train to Italy.

So Gertrude and I found ourselves stranded in a very expensive Italian hotel with hardly any money, just enough for a few days, because the quartet expected to receive some pay soon after arrival. Since we had no money to eat in the hotel and pay the bill, we had to smuggle cheap food into our room and try not to leave crumbs around. Gertrude, who speaks some Italian, persuaded the Italian agent to let us have some money to make the journey home. So we slunk away back to London in a very depressed mood.

That trip was the last straw. Dick had always made the travel arrangements for the quartet and I was furious at the chaos he had caused. I could see other problems coming up and decided I had had enough. I did a few more engagements with the group but it was all over after the Milan fiasco and I wanted a change. I looked around for other possibilities and handed in my notice on April 10th 1951. The very day after I last worked with the quartet I started with Tito Burns.

6.

a lesson in bop

Strangely enough, on the last day I worked with Ray Ellington, something happened which began a completely new phase for the quartet: it successfully auditioned to become the regular band on a radio show that was then just about to go out on the air. At first the show was called 'Crazy People' but, after the first series in 1951, the BBC agreed to change the title to what Spike Milligan, Peter Sellers, Harry Secombe and the others who had devised the show wanted. From that time, it became famous as 'The Goon Show', a brilliant comedy programme that brought something entirely new to broadcasting and greatly influenced later classics such as 'Monty Python'. It made the Goons – Sellers, Milligan and Secombe – famous as comedians and it did great things for the popularity of the Ray Ellington Quartet, which was featured in its own music spot every week. Also, Ray often had parts written for him (usually as Chief Ellinga or the Red Bladder) in the script.

Ray was a good friend of Sellers and some time before that audition, the quartet had been invited to one of Sellers' parties. Spike Milligan was there, we played and it was a very jolly affair. At some point Sellers and the others took turns playing and fooling around with Ray's drums. Everyone had a good time. I don't know whether that occasion had any connection with our doing the audition later but the quartet, like the Goons, had an element of crazy fun, so someone may have felt that what we liked to do would fit with what the Goons wanted to do in radio comedy.

The audition was the funniest thing I had ever come across. It was hilarious seeing the Goons doing their zany stuff and I was sorry, for that reason, that I wouldn't be doing the actual shows. We made a complete pilot show for the BBC Governors with all the comedy and the music, recorded before an audience in the old Paris Cinema in Lower Regent Street which the BBC had taken over since the war. At that time there was also a fourth goon, Michael Bentine, who took part in the pilot show and the early broadcasts, but later dropped out.

After I had given in my notice there were still engagements with Ray booked until the day I was scheduled to leave. We did a cabaret at a police dance in Porchester Hall in west London – Harry Secombe was involved in that. Then there was a short tour: Manchester, Bolton, Leeds, Warrington, Southsea – the usual scurrying from place to place. Then broadcasts and a concert at the London Palladium. Then more touring: Wigan, Liverpool, Manchester, Stockport, Winsford, Derby, Swindon and back to London. So I was busy with the group right up to the end. In fact we hardly rested all the time I was with the band, apart from a couple of weeks off as holiday each year.

After I left, a bass player named Lennie Harrison took my place, He was Ray's friend but he didn't stay long. He didn't have an amplified bass so that altered the balance in the group and, in any case, he really didn't play the instrument well. I think people noticed the difference. After Lennie, Peter McGurk took over. Ray kept playing and bandleading for many years. Dick Katz stayed with the quartet until 1959 and then worked in a theatrical agency. Laurie Deniz left two years after I did. He became ill, drifted out of music and did labouring work, although he did continue to play sometimes in various groups. Even during the time we were together in the quartet, Laurie had problems. He smoked marijuana and maybe eventually it affected him, because he became a schizophrenic. At one time, when he had no playing work, he did a job at my home, fixing the gateposts. Sometimes he would be in hospital. It was sad and, as I said earlier, I was close with his family. They were good friends.

I joined Tito Burns and his Sextet on Sunday May 7th 1951. I didn't know much about them except that they had plenty of work, were popular around the country, and were jazz oriented. The word must have got around that I had given in my notice to Ray, and when Tito heard about this he asked me to join because his bass player had just left to join Ted Heath. His sextet had sometimes been on the same bill as the Ellington Quartet at concerts and, in the week I joined Tito, *Melody Maker* reported him as saying that, 'through these contacts I have acquired the greatest admiration for Cole's terrific musical and comedy attributes.'

Tito's band toured just as extensively as the Ellington quartet had. As soon as the last tour with Ray had come to an end I was off on the road again. My diary for that time lists the dates: Wolverhampton, Manchester, Ashton, Rhyl, Oldham, Nelson, Scarborough, Hanley, Ramsgate, Bedford, Whitchurch, Leeds, Leicester – usually playing just for a night or for a few days. I can just about read other fading, pencilled diary entries: Southsea, Aylesbury, Southend, Norwich, Nottingham, the Corn Exchange at Wisbech, Newcastle, Leith, Aberdeen, Inverness, Kirkcaldy,

Scarborough, Stockton. That's how it went. My bags were always packed. Then we started to go abroad too.

Tito Burns' Sextet is an almost forgotten bit of the history of jazz in Britain, but it attracted good audiences and Tito was serious about trying to get the message of modern jazz across to the public. It was around the time of Club Eleven and while Tito kept himself apart from the Club Eleven crowd, like them he had a mission. He wanted to play bebop but he had the idea of dressing it up to make it attractive to audiences who would have been driven away by a pure diet of Parker's and Gillespie's music. The idea was something like the one Charlie Ventura had in America at much the same time with his 'bop for the people' small band – to present modern jazz that would be entertaining and in a show with plenty of variety. That was part of what the Ray Ellington Quartet had been about but Tito and his band didn't have much of the quartet's crazy humour. He tried to make the show exotic and mix ballads, novelty numbers and jazz pieces in a sort of broad entertainment with a bit of fun and a bit of serious stuff.

Tito played squeeze box, piano accordion. He was one of the very few musicians who have tried seriously to play modern jazz on the instrument. He had a good technique and could get his fingers around the complicated, fast lines of bop tunes and solos impressively. He understood the idiom and in his own way played quite well. I knew nothing about his history when I joined him but he had been leading his sextet since 1947 and the personnel tended to be very stable over the years. He always hired people who understood and played in the modern style.

Alwyn 'Albert' Hall, the trumpeter, who came from Wales, was a lovely player. He wasn't a bop man, strictly speaking, but he had a beautiful sound and could play whatever was written for him. We always had very elaborate arrangements although Tito wasn't an arranger himself. The scores were provided by Ronnie Price, the sextet's pianist, and he was very talented that way, making full use of all the group's instrumental resources. There were always a couple of saxophones and one advantage of the accordion in the front line was that its big, loud, rich chords supported the trumpet and saxes very effectively. It could add a bit of breadth to the sound of the group, beef it up harmonically and, with the piano, create the sense of a really huge sound in the ensembles. Sometimes, because of Ronnie's clever arrangements, the sextet sounded almost like a big band, as can be heard on many of its records.

Strictly speaking, it was a sextet plus Terry Devon, Tito's wife, who was always an important part of the group. She had first made a name for herself as a singer with Billy Thorburn's dance band while in her teens. A decade or so later, with Tito's sextet, she sang ballads with her attractive, light voice and sometimes used it instrumentally alongside the trumpet and saxes in the arrangements. She was also featured on novelties such as 'A Lesson in Bop' where the vocal line probably summed up how the band saw itself in relation to some of its audiences:

> Don't blow your top
> Listen to what we say
> Dig this jive
> We'll try to prove to you
> Bop's OK!

Sometimes Terry and Tito sang together in the slick boy-girl bop duet style that Jackie Cain and Roy Kral popularised with Ventura's band in the States. She was a good singer and the comedy bits in the repertoire would usually involve her and me. We did a version of Nellie Lutcher's hit, 'Fine Brown Frame', and of course I was the one with the fine, brown frame, being the only brown person in the band. Terry and I shared that number, with a lot of comedy banter between us. She had a nice personality and, like Tito, she understood and enjoyed the modern sounds of the time, so Harold Davison promoted the two of them as 'Mr. and Mrs. Bop'.

The drummer, Derek Price – Ronnie's brother – was very powerful but a bit on the heavy side for my liking. You might say he *drove* the band and it certainly could swing a bit. Then there were the two saxophones. Altoist Jimmy Chester was like some other bop-inclined English saxophonists of the time: sounding head over heels in his solos, finding it a bit hard to get his ideas across and trying to get his fingers around an awful lot of notes. Rex Morris, the tenor player, was more fluent. We used to call him Sexy Rexy because he was definitely one for the girls. He was an ebullient little guy and liked a bit of fun. But among the soloists, Albert Hall stood out a mile, as can be heard, for example, on 'Festival Hall', featuring his lead and solo playing. We recorded that for Esquire in July 1951, along with 'A Lesson in Bop' and two other numbers.

Soon after that recording session for Carlo Krahmer, Jimmy Chester was replaced by Don Savage on alto and tenor saxes. Don was a good, earnest musician, rather on the serious side and very slim and slender-featured. He was an impressive soloist, much better than Jimmy. But, in general, the personnel didn't change much, probably because it was a secure job if you were with Tito. He always had work around the dance halls because the musical policy was very carefully judged. As with Ray Ellington, we didn't play for dancing, but we would do a kind of cabaret spot in the interval when the dance band took its break. Sometimes we had a whole show to ourselves and occasionally there were big jazz concerts where the sextet was featured alongside other bands.

I remember little of the sextet's music now, except when I'm reminded of it from records, but there were all the intricate, quite exciting bebop things with short improvised solos well integrated into the arrangements, as well as popular songs of the day which Terry sang. She was very attractive and always wore lovely dresses on stage, so that created the glamour. And where there was a chance to insert a bit of comedy, fun or novelty we would take that chance and do something. It didn't strike me that there were any comedians in the band, except for Rex who was always a joker. So maybe I brought a few ideas that way into what we did.

I had to fit into a musical set-up that was already well established and so it wasn't a matter of together working out a style and a means of musical expression, as it had been with the Caribbean Trio and then with Ray Ellington. Tito had his musical ideas and the other guys in the band had mainly been with him for some time. So they shared the same assumptions about what the band was trying to do musically and they were used to the sound they produced together. Playing in such an explicitly bebop-oriented way was new for me.

Also, when you have played with a group for a long time you develop a particular sound you know is good and which fits well with the group. You know when it's right and everything gels musically. It takes time to get to that point. The feeling instilled in you by music is a subtle, elusive thing and good, true musicians are always aware of that and react to it. In the Ray Ellington Quartet we were used to the feel of making music together. Every group has its own feeling. With another group it's bound to be completely different even if the instrumentation is the same. The sounds coming at you are not the same and you have to respond differently to make it right. A very different instrumentation or a different size of group alters things and even the different way the band is set up on stage can do it, but basically the musical personalities determine everything.

When I joined Tito I almost literally hit the ground running. I'd just finished the last tour with Ray and then, straight away, I was on the road with the sextet. As far as I remember, I knew nothing about their music beforehand: only that the sextet was one of the good, busy, recognised jazz groups, that it would be something different and that I would be able to handle whatever they were doing. One of the first jobs we did was a concert in St. Pancras in London and then we were off on tour, racing all over the country. There wasn't time to do anything like sit down and learn the book, get to know the band's repertoire. Fortunately, the arrangements were written out and we always rehearsed. So I would learn the pieces then. If you're used to that sort of thing it is routine. We were always working so I would see a new piece for the first time at rehearsal and then we'd play it at the gig that night.

Tito had been on active service throughout most of the war and maybe that was a reason why we did a lot of work at armed forces bases abroad. With finance provided by the Americans, we toured NATO bases in Germany and saw how the country was being rebuilt at a tremendous pace after the wartime devastation. Somewhere near Stuttgart I noticed people building a house: they had completed about a quarter of it. A couple of days later we passed it again and it looked almost completely built. They had worked night and day. So thorough, and such hard workers! Hamburg too: it had been smashed to smithereens but now it was all being cleared up. I don't know how they did it so quickly.

The German tour was in the depths of winter and we brought the New Year in at Mainz. The local musicians put on a terrific spread for us and the drink flowed freely. Late at night, after much celebrating, we hung around each others' necks and said things like, 'We must never fight again. Our countries must never go to war again. It was all so stupid. Never again! Friends forever!' It was a fantastically friendly atmosphere and very emotional. This was only a few years after the war had ended and there was still a sense of renewing contact across Europe after everything that had happened. Having fought each other for years we could relax together again with music and socialise. It was quite something, very significant.

We toured bases where American servicemen were stationed and things must have changed somewhat on the race front by then. Anyway, I didn't have any problems like those that had arisen years before with Johnny Claes' band. We travelled by coach around southern Germany. And in the package was a very good, versatile, up and coming young comedian and entertainer named Bruce Forsyth who was travelling with his wife, Penny Calvert. He played piano and they danced and sang together. They were a talented act and she was a sweet, lovely girl, so it was sad when later they broke up.

Brucie and his wife were also with us when we went to Malta around Christmas 1952 to play for the British forces based there. All I remember about that trip is the strangeness of it. We stayed outside Valetta, the capital, and a car would come to take us to town. There were a couple of night clubs where jazz was played and a Maltese drummer there was so good that I persuaded him to come to London to make a career. The island was hot and dry and in the mornings we enjoyed the sunshine. But the beaches were strictly out of bounds. The sands were full of mines from the wartime defences so it wasn't safe to go there.

Nowadays there are few images in my memory from all that touring with Tito. One is from when we went to north Africa for six weeks to play at British forces bases out in the desert. We performed one night at a camp where the servicemen marooned on their tour of duty, surrounded by sand, hadn't seen any women for maybe a couple of years. When Terry walked on stage they erupted. The noise was deafening and it took some time for them to calm down. Of course, we stayed on the base overnight before moving on and I remember the stillness. Out in the desert the dusk comes quickly and it gets impenetrably dark so that the atmosphere can be strange. The camp was surrounded by a big fence to keep marauders out and I can still remember the sound of the guard dogs howling mournfully around the perimeter fence all through the small hours.

Tito wasn't a forceful personality but he was a proficient leader and knew what he wanted. All the band parts were carefully numbered and he would have lists of numbers to fix the order of what we would play during a gig. On stage, after each piece, he'd call out the number of the next one and we would dutifully put it up on the music stand and play it. We had uniforms, suits, and the whole perform-ance was routinised. Everyone read music well so we didn't have to have elaborate rehearsals. We would just get to the gig early and run through a few things to sort out any difficulties.

The best part was travelling, getting around and seeing places and chatting on the journeys. Rexy was fun to be with and Brucie and his wife were also garrulous on the tours. I usually travelled with the rest of the band at that time. Around Germany and on some of the other foreign trips we would travel in a coach provided by the armed services whose bases we were playing. In England, the band had its own small bus with storage room for the instru-ments and a few seats. We always had the same driver who also looked after the instruments. Not everyone in the sex-tet travelled that way – the bus was not big enough for us all and Tito and Terry travelled separately in style – but I would never allow my instrument to go anywhere I didn't go. It lay on the back seat of the bus near me. But it was a cold way to get around. The bus had no proper heating and, at night, coming back after gigs, I would curl up feeling frozen, trying to sleep.

Musically, life with Tito was far less satisfying than what I had been involved with before. Being in the sextet moved me into a new musical idiom because Tito was committed to bebop in a way that the Ray Ellington Quartet hadn't been. Most musicians are steeped in a certain style and they don't move into a completely different idiom. They don't have the chance to do that. But classical musicians have to play different styles all the time. They read a part and interpret it as the composer intended. They don't have to use their personal interpretation of anything. They have to follow the conductor. So they are skilled in playing many different idioms but the inspiration of the music is not coming, as it were, from them. It comes from the composer and the conductor. It felt a bit like that with the Tito Burns Sextet. It wasn't my music in any real sense. I just played it. So that's probably why most of it has not stayed in my memory.

Tito Burns was certainly a phenomenon. Although he wasn't charismatic, his band managed to be commercially viable and kept busy for many years. There was no other bop band with an accordian and I think it was the instrument itself that people went to hear, and the unusual way it was being used. And with Terry Devon as a featured attraction and all the careful attention to putting on a good, varied show, there was always something to keep the audience interested.

In August 1953, after two years with the sextet, I left. Tito ran the band for another couple of years and then disbanded and retired from the life of endless touring. His sextet had achieved a lot of recognition but he felt that change was in the air in the popular music world and he had gone as far as he could with the small group format he had worked with for eight years. Terry stayed at home to raise a

family and Tito gave up his squeeze box and became a successful agent and impresario who brought many top
American musicians to play in Britain over the years. Later
he became Head of Variety Programming for London
Weekend Television.

But you rarely see his name in the jazz reference books
now. He kept himself and his career apart from the Club
Eleven crowd so he didn't have a place in that group which
has become a little bit of the history of modern jazz in
Britain. Also, he was almost the only bop accordionist and
probably, for purist jazz followers, the instrument was never
taken seriously, so what he did seems a curiosity now.

I left Tito because eventually I needed a change, maybe
something more satisfying musically and something that
would move my career on. The first thing that came up was
a short engagement accompanying Rose Murphy at a series
of concerts in theatres around the country. I joined her on
August 17th and we appeared first at the Empire Theatre,
Edinburgh. She was a big star and the work was very good
exposure for me because she sang and played piano just
with bass accompaniment: the theatres were filled with her
enthusiastic fans and, since only the two of us were on
stage, the bass had plenty of prominence. The American
bassist Major Holley had played with her immediately
before and I knew him because we had sometimes worked
in the same clubs, so he had recommended me for the job
with Rose when he left.

She had a very distinctive, almost childlike voice and
Melody Maker wrote, at the time I joined her, about 'her tiny
thread of a voice and her butterfly fingering of the keyboard'. She used to bring a wooden board on stage with her
and pump her foot up and down on it as she played to
sound out the beat. So we swung hard when she wanted to
and didn't miss having a drummer. She was quite a large

woman and I sometimes had to ferry her around in my lit-tle Vauxhall 10, which was quite a squash.

The period with Rose was just a month or so. In the longer term I had the idea that I wanted to play music I was helping to shape, not just read a part and do what was required as with Tito. So I thought I would try setting up a group of my own. I got in touch with Lauderic Caton again and he agreed to join me in a new group. We invited anoth-er guitarist too, a friend of Lauderic's named Ronnie Wilkins, so the two of them could exchange lead and rhythm guitar roles. A pianist, a chubby guy named Jack Gordon, completed the quartet, which I called the Dominoes. I decided that, just as in the Caribbean Trio (and with Rose Murphy), we didn't need drums.

In a way it was an attempt to get back to the feeling I had had with the Caribbean Trio. For me, that group and then the quartet with Ray were the tops, the most enjoyable things I ever did in the whole of my career. But, of course, it was impossible to recapture the feeling of the Caribbean Trio and the style had to be different. Jack Gordon used an electronic keyboard which didn't have the quality of a piano and, as a player, he certainly wasn't in the same class as Dick Katz. Ronnie Wilkins was mainly into Latin American music and so was Jack, in a way. They were not really jazz-oriented although we managed to play a few standards.

We played in London clubs including one in New Compton Street which used to be the old Fullado – among the earliest haunts of British modern jazz. One night, some rowdies came up to the bandstand to cause trouble. But Jack Gordon was a tough character, short but stocky and strong. He did weightlifting and kept very fit. He grabbed these thugs by the collar, pushed them through the crowd and frogmarched them outside on to the pavement before they knew what was happening. Jack was someone who didn't stand any nonsense and he was a useful guy to have around sometimes.

It was clear that to get enough work and make a success the music had to be more commercial than before. I decided we needed a singer but, despite a lot of auditions and try-outs, we had great difficulty getting someone with a good style who could sing in tune. Eventually, after many disappointments, we found the perfect vocalist. She was the daughter of Leslie 'Jiver' Hutchinson and her name was Elaine Delmar.

Her first job with us was a one month engagement at a German night club, the Club Ecstase in Bad Harzburg in the Harz Mountains. She was about sixteen and, although she had worked a bit with her father, it was her very first public engagement with a band as a professional singer, so I think it's fair to say that we started off her career. Of course, she was a real find. She had wonderful pitch, a great style and a fresh, vibrant voice and, although she has never received as much recognition as she deserves, over the years she has become one of the finest jazz-oriented singers around.

The experience in Germany was very good. Elaine went over well with audiences and met her first boyfriend there. She was romantically inclined and the guys all fell for her. She had a nice personality and, of course, was very pretty and attractive. Gertrude and Sandy came over for some of the time and I even got to play some tennis at the local club. On the way back, the band worked for a couple of nights at a lakeside restaurant on the outskirts of Hamburg where there was a wonderful fireworks display over the lake.

In fact the Club Ecstase engagement was the high point of the Dominoes' existence. Elaine only stayed with the band for that month. Then it was back to looking for another good vocalist, someone who could sing our arrangements in close harmony with the instruments rather than just rely on us backing her. We usually had to hire not very experienced singers because we couldn't afford well established ones, so we were always looking for promising new people.

The group also did a tour in north Africa as part of an entertainment package, much like the one the Tito Burns Sextet had had with Bruce Forsyth and Penny Calvert. Our partner in the package was an American comedian, Vic Perry, who featured a pickpocket act. He would invite people from the audience to come onstage, chatter away to them, then produce out of thin air, as it seemed, something that had been in the victim's pocket and say, 'Oh, is this yours?', while doing something else. He'd take off someone's braces without them knowing, or even a shirt. His act always got a lot of laughs.

We flew with Vic Perry to north Africa in a tiny unpressurised plane but he became quite seriously ill on the way. He was hugely fat and had a very dicky heart. So we had a difficult time with him and the plane had to fly as low as possible so that he wouldn't have another bout of illness with his heart before we reached the destination. We managed to survive the travelling and played at a string of military bases. I remember staying in a beautiful hotel in Tripoli in Libya, and seeing Rabat in Morocco, as well as Casablanca. But, as in Malta, along the coast there were all the mined beaches that had to be avoided.

The heat was almost unbearable. Travelling along the north African coast in the bus with windows wide open was like being in an oven and the hot wind burned our faces. At that time I played cello as well as bass to add to the variety. At one place I set up my cello on stage ready for the concert and went away to get prepared. After a short while I heard a loud bang from the stage. The back of the cello had warped, opened up and blown half off. The heat had dried it out in just a few minutes and the cello was unplayable for the rest of the tour and had to be reglued when I came home. At some time on one of those Africa trips, my bass suffered a disaster too. It had been loaded in the luggage compartment of the plane with mailbags piled on top of it so that the sound post had been pushed through the wood, breaking the instrument. Over the years that bass has certainly been in the wars.

The Dominoes ran down as a group as the work became less and other playing opportunities took its place in those mid-1950s years – short-term musical associations and occasional gigs. Around that time, I worked with a vibraphonist named Reg Wale at weekends. He had a regular gig at a tennis club in Hampstead and each week different musicians would come by and play. It was very relaxed and informal and Reg was a good player so we had lovely times. Lionel Evans, a property developer, ran the club and lived just across the road from it. After playing we would usually be invited to his place for 'drinkies' and he always treated us wonderfully. The tennis club building itself was remarkable for the fact that it had a tree growing inside it, right through the roof, which had been erected around the tree; there were a few problems when it rained, as I recall.

Also in the mid-1950s, I started to work frequently on and off with the pianist Alan Clare at the Studio Club, in Swallow Street in Piccadilly, and then later at the Star Club in Wardour Street. It wasn't a regular job for me, because I played with a lot of different musicians in different places during those years. Of course, if you are not committed to a regular band you take the best work available at any particular time. I had worked with Alan before when I played a short engagement with Harry Hayes' sextet in the late 1940s and he was the pianist. But he liked to be his own leader. He was an excellent solo pianist – that's essentially the way he worked all his professional life from the 1950s – and being resident at the Studio Club and the Star Club he could invite whoever he liked to come along to accompany him.

He had a wonderful harmonic sense and lovely technique and his legato playing was outstanding. Certainly he had plenty of ideas and a style of his own. But he remained a musicians' musician and never gained a big popular reputation because he didn't record much, preferred to work as a solo pianist rather than become a sideman in any popular jazz group and didn't have the urge to travel with his music. He just loved to play in an intimate club atmosphere and when he found a good environment to work in – somewhere where he felt really comfortable – he was happy to stay with it and play to a familiar audience.

The Studio Club, where Alan worked for a long time, certainly had atmosphere. It was a 'day' (evening) club, not a night club, and the clientele were mainly artists and people from the music world and the Soho film world. I played there with him, on and off, for many years through to the 1960s. The Star Club, where I worked with Alan in the late 1950s, had a more typical clientele. Sometimes guest singers would join us on the bandstand, Kenny Lynch and Rosemary Squires among them. And the Star was where I first played with the Scottish drummer Bobby Orr who would become my regular rhythm section partner in the coming years.

Right from the beginning I liked Bobby's playing very much. His rhythmic sense and ability to hold a tempo are tremendous. For me, as a bass player, one of the first things you appreciate is a drummer who, once he has started a tempo, will finish at exactly that tempo. You'd be amazed how many drummers cannot do that. If the tempo stays solid I can relax on the beat and concentrate on playing inventively. But if the tempo isn't firm it upsets me and I can't play so well. Bobby comes from Lanarkshire and was brought up on pipe bands there – marching bands where the tempo has to be strict and steady. He gets the feel of the swing and the steady beat and his playing is definite, positive and clearcut. He used to play trumpet too but after he damaged his lip he concentrated on drums. On a social level, we got on well from the start. He is a nice person, good to be with, and likes a joke. Today, he is as busy as ever, always in demand.

All kinds of musicians would drop by at the Star Club to sit in. One of these, and by far the most notable musically, came one evening when Bobby Orr and I were playing there with Alan. The visitor was a sharply dressed Jamaican alto saxophone player named Joe Harriott. We played together as a quartet and he sounded magnificent. He was powerful, aggressive, fluent and supremely confident as a soloist in a way that was very unusual among jazz improvisers in Britain at that time. That evening at the Star Club was the first time I played with Harriott but it certainly wasn't the first occasion I had heard him. He already had a big reputation as a jazz improviser, full of passion and technically amazing.

My first experience of hearing Joe – one that always stayed clear in my mind – happened long before. It was at one of the first concerts I played with Tito Burns in 1951 at St. Pancras Town Hall in London. Harriott was working with the relief band on the bill with us there that evening, Ozzie Da Costa's West Indian group, which Joe had come to Britain with earlier that year. The trombonist and composer Herman Wilson, who was then also in Da Costa's band, told me years later how excited the guys had been to see me playing with Tito. There had been a lot of talk about me back in Kingston but no-one had known exactly what I was doing in my career, and there I was working with the other band. Anyway, shortly after that St. Pancras gig, Joe left Da Costa and decided to stay in Britain. So that was the beginning of his career here. When I heard him at St. Pancras in 1951 he stood out a mile from the other musicians. He was already a very impressive player and he got better and better as the years went by.

In the seven years between that gig and the time I met him at the Star Club, he had worked with a lot of bands. One of the first was led by the Jamaican trumpeter Pete Pitterson. I had also worked alongside Pete at various times. We were both in Harry Hayes' sextet, for example, playing for a couple of weeks at a restaurant in Wardour Street in the late 1940s, and there were other occasions. He was a pleasant guy and played particularly well on ballads, with a good sound. But he worked a lot in the black clubs in London so our paths didn't cross much.

Harriott had also been a member of Ronnie Scott's orchestra and the drummer Allan Ganley's quartet. But his main musical association in the years before we met was with the small groups led by another modern jazz drummer, Tony Kinsey. More than anything, it was regular work around London with Kinsey – especially in well-known jazz venues like Jeff Kruger's Flamingo Club – that had made a lot of people aware of how outstanding Harriott was.

It must have been March 1958 when he walked into the Star Club. He had decided he was ready, at last, to form a group of his own and that evening he asked me if I would like to join it. I didn't hesitate, just as I hadn't hesitated 16 years before, when Johnny Claes had walked into a club where I was working and asked me the same sort of question. I knew Harriott was a jazz improviser way beyond the ordinary run of players, one of the very best – maybe the best – in Britain. So there and then I joined what became the Joe Harriott Quintet. I think it was on that same evening that Joe also invited Bobby Orr to join.

Musically, working with Joe was obviously going to be something fresh and challenging. At first, what struck me most about him was the way he had so completely absorbed the bebop idiom. Later he became an entirely unique player with a style unmistakeably his own but at that time he was the nearest thing to Charlie Parker that I had heard in Britain. It wasn't like Tito Burns and his group who had learned something at second hand and skilfully adapted it to make presentable entertainment. Joe lived and breathed Parker's music. In a way he lived *in* it. Bebop was his language at that time. It was the way he expressed himself and he was totally at ease with it. Nobody else produced that glorious sound he made. I think he said, years later, remembering his early style, that he had 'just been a Charlie Parker player', as though he was dismissing it in a way, but that was the phase he went through to master bop. Charlie was his mentor. Joining Joe's new band meant throwing in my lot very clearly with that musical idiom. I would be part of a group that created this music in its own way and was committed one hundred per cent to it.

It's hard to credit now what a schism there was in the late 1940s and through most of the 1950s between the modern jazz musicians and fans, on the one hand, and the traditionalists, on the other, who preferred some or all of the earlier styles that had been the way everyone understood jazz before Parker, Gillespie and the others changed everything. The jazz world became polarised. The so-called revivalists came up at the end of the 1940s: Graeme Bell, George Webb, Ken Colyer, Humphrey Lyttleton and people like that. And, on the other hand, there were the Club Eleven people, the ardent boppers. That was when the big divide began. The Ray Ellington Quartet had definitely been in the middle and I tried always just to be on the side of good music. Music occurs in many different styles. It's purely a question of what is relevant for you, what makes you tick personally. You can't pass judgment on things like that.

Dixieland, for example, doesn't turn me on, even though the Graeme Bells were very earnest and when I started out in jazz I collected a few dixieland records – Bob Crosby and that sort of thing. On the other hand, the existence of the hard drugs scene kept me away from some of the modern jazz circles. I didn't want anything to do with that. But to complete your musical education you have to embrace and learn about all types of music and then see what appeals to you and what you feel at home with. I found I was very at home with Harriott's music as it developed in the years after 1958. In fact the Joe Harriott Quintet became a musical home for me for about the next seven years. Those years gave me some of the greatest musical adventures of my life, as well as some of the greatest heartaches.

7.

blue Harriott

Joe Harriott had secured a residency at the Marquee Club, downstairs from the Rex Cinema on the corner of Poland Street and Oxford Street. Such was his reputation that he had got the booking to play there with his new group even before the band had been unveiled to the public or the personnel had been fixed. The Marquee itself was a new venture. It had been set up by the National Jazz Federation to provide a central London venue where all kinds of jazz and blues could be presented and it opened in the spring of 1958 with a broad musical policy. On most nights, traditional and mainstream jazz, blues and rhythm-and-blues were the staples, but at weekends there was modern jazz, and Joe obtained a regular booking for Saturdays.

Having chosen Bobby Orr and me to join him, he completed the quintet with Hank Shaw on trumpet as his front line partner and Harry South on piano. Joe was then 29 and the others were around the same age, with me as the veteran at 44. Hank was very definitely a bopper, a self-taught musician and one of the better bebop-style players at that time. He had played in Oscar Rabin's dance orchestra during the war. Later he became a founding member of the

Club Eleven group and worked with Vic Lewis's big band and with Ronnie Scott in the mid-1950s. I don't think he was all that healthy and he wasn't very strong – sort of wiry and on the skinny side physically. That had an effect on his sound but he had a good grasp of the bop idiom and in his own way he contributed most, apart from Joe, to the style of the new quintet. Harry South had less of an influence that way but he was more of a solid citizen type than Hank. He had his own style too and quite a good way of playing.

Harry was also an arranger and composer and had previously written music for Ronnie Scott's mid-1950s band. He composed a bright, attractive tune 'Strollin' South' for the quintet and we also used pieces Joe had written, including his old riff blues 'Just Goofin'' which became the group's signature tune and 'Count Twelve', another blues with a swaggering swing inspired by the feeling of the Basie band.

Overall, the style of the group was what people called hard bop at that time – not the fast and furious bebop that modern jazz had started with around a decade before, but a more direct and bluesy music. In contrast to the 'cool', soft 'West Coast' jazz popular a few years before and mainly produced by white Californian musicians, hard bop had a tough, virile sound and was mainly associated with black New York bands. The soul-jazz style of Horace Silver was a big influence on our quintet and we used several of his tunes, like 'Sister Sadie' and 'Señor Blues'. But we didn't copy anyone. We found our own style that we felt comfortable with, one that suited Joe and that each of us in the group could contribute to in our different ways.

Joe never wrote parts for the instruments. We had guides to set out the chord changes but never scores. He would sketch out the music, usually just the themes and ideas for the ensemble playing and we would rehearse the pieces and put our own interpretation on what he had written. That was always the way, even in later years when the music was very different from the hard bop we were playing at the end of the 1950s. But Joe always knew what he wanted musically. He was a strong leader that way and, as far as presenting the band went, he did it in a very personal way.

He would typically say something like: 'Now, I would like to play for you Thelonious Monk's 'Round Midnight',' or whatever the piece was. Always 'I'. He never used the word 'we'. It would never be: 'And now *we* would like to play for you...' He talked like that right from the beginning and I always found it odd, astonishing really, because we were a tight group musically and were all contributing. But that was something you got used to, like a lot of aspects of the way he was personally. He did his job and people liked it. I suppose most people don't worry about things like that. But I found out very quickly that Joe was a man apart, a difficult person in all sorts of ways. The effects of all that came out much later.

Playing with him regularly I recognised, even more than I had before, his huge talent and his sheer consistency as a jazz improviser. All his best records show a quality which, in my view, stands up against any other alto player. In performance he seemed as though he was striving to express himself to the limit and you could feel a great tension in his playing. His technical fluency always allowed him to play with massive confidence, power and aggression. But sometimes on slow ballads there was a tender quality in his improvisations and his alto would have a lovely, almost plaintive tone.

We rehearsed at the Marquee and began to play regularly there. But we had to miss a couple of Saturdays at the club because Joe had also fixed up a booking abroad for the group in that first month: a short residency at a place called the Storyville Club in Frankfurt where we played for about two weeks. Bobby Orr couldn't manage to do the trip so we

Above 'One of the satisfactory organisations in this Island': Kingston Glee Singers Society, 1925. Seated, left to right: George Goode, Hilda Goode, unknown, Ethel Marson, Sam Kitchin (photo from E. Marson, *George Davis Goode*).

Left Coleridge Goode, late 1940s (photo courtesy of *Daily Mail*, London)

'Come to America with me': Django Reinhardt relaxing at CG's house in London, January 1946, just before his disastrous US trip (photo by Coleridge Goode).

'Some people thought it was very irreverent to be jazzing up the national anthem': Django and Stéphane Grappelli reunited in the recording studio, London, January 1946; CG on bass, Allan Hodgkiss, guitar.

Above 'Something for every sophisticated taste': Stéphane Grappelli with George Shearing on piano, guitarist Dave Goldberg, CG, and Ray Ellington at the drums, on film in 1946.
Below Ray Ellington Quartet (CG, Dick Katz, Ray Ellington, Laurie Deniz) broadcasting in Hilversum, Holland, 1949 (photo by J. H. C. Vermeulen).

Above 'An unusual background which had him screwed up for a lifetime': Ray Ellington (centre) with Dick Katz and Lauderic Caton (Photo Chadel, Nice). *Below left* Tito Burns c1950 (photo courtesy of *Jazz Journal International*). *Below right* Ray Ellington Quartet c.1948. Top to bottom: CG, Dick Katz, Lauderic Caton, Ray Ellington.

Left 'A great style and a fresh, vibrant voice': Elaine Delmar singing with The Dominoes, Club Ecstase, Bad Harzburg, in the mid-1950s (Herbert Ahrens photo).

Below 'Some of the greatest musical adventures of my life': Joe Harriott Quintet in rehearsal, probably late 1959. Left to right: Harry South, CG, Hank Shaw, Joe Harriott, Bobby Orr (Photography 33 photo).

Above left 'He channelled all that longing through his music': Joe Harriott (photo by Patrick Gwynne-Jones). *Above right* CG with Pat Smythe: 'I loved hearing him play, whatever the context'. ICA, London, 1960s. *Below* Left to right: Bobby Orr, Hank Shaw, Joe Harriott, Frank Holder and Harry South. Storyville Club, Frankfurt, 1959. CG is obscured behind Harriott (Herbert Gerhold photo).

Above Shake Keane, CG and Dave Brubeck's bassist Gene Wright, London c. 1961 (photo by Russ Allen)

Left 'The Harold and Eric Show': Prime Minister Harold Wilson's joke amuses comedian Eric Morecambe and CG, at Wilson's resignation party, 1976 (photo by Joe Bulaitis).

Bottom Making music at 10 Downing Street, 1976, at Harold Wilson's resignation party, with Peter Shade on flute and vibes and Leslie Paul on piano (photo by Joe Bulaitis).

Above With Michael Garrick, Colin Barnes (seated) and (at rear) Joe Harriott, at a recording session for Michael's *October Woman* album in November 1964 (photo by Harley Usill).

Above right 'Travel. it's part of the life': on a Michael Garrick gig with all the usual gear in the late 1970s.

Bottom Cole and Gertrude.

had to use another drummer, Benny Goodman.

I travelled to Germany in my usual way, driving my car. Benny Goodman came with me as he didn't have to take his whole kit. He used some drums that were already over there at the club. Benny's real name was David but at some point, unfortunately perhaps, he had become known by the name of the very famous American clarinettist. He only worked with the quintet on that trip. As a drummer he was competent enough and had worked with fine modern jazz players such as saxophonist Don Rendell and trumpeter Dizzy Reece. But as soon as Bobby Orr was available again, shortly after the Frankfurt trip, Joe wanted Bobby in the quintet and he became the regular drummer. Benny took a job playing on the liner *Mauretania*. Later there was a brief spell when a black Liverpool-born drummer, Tommy Jones, played with the Harriott quintet, but Bobby worked on and off with the group throughout its existence, except for a time when the great Phil Seamen held the drum chair. But that's something to talk about later.

The Frankfurt engagement was a good start for the quintet and we settled down to working together quite easily. The Storyville was a jazz club so audiences came expecting to hear modern jazz and were reasonably knowledgeable about it. They liked our style and group sound and, of course, Joe's fiery playing.

Hank Shaw's girlfriend followed us to Frankfurt to be with him. Motor scooters were popular at that time and she rode her scooter all the way from London. In Frankfurt, during the day, you could see her on this noisy little bike skidding along the streets around the Storyville Club with Hank perched on the back clinging on for dear life. He was a character in all sorts of ways and always short of money. But I didn't see a lot of him except on the stand. In fact that was the way it was with the whole group, as far as I was concerned. We didn't spend much time together. I discovered a little eaterie across the road from the club, where they served an excellent kind of German sausage with potato salad. I had never eaten that before and it tasted marvellous washed down with a good beer. So I developed a taste for it and I'd go there on my own each night after the gig and have a fine meal.

Back in London, we all went our separate ways socially apart from when we played or rehearsed the music. In the breaks between sets at the Marquee we would all go to the Coach and Horses pub in Poland Street and Joe would hold forth there. That was where I first developed a taste for Special Brew beer: before that it had just been water or soft drinks. But that was more or less the extent of the socialising. We came together to play the music and that was the focal point. Once we had finished the final set for the night I would be packing up and setting off home. When I wasn't working I wanted to spend as much time as I could with the family. Hank would always have his girl friend in tow and Harry had his wife. In fact, he met her at the Marquee. I think she was a model and she used to come in there regularly.

Off the bandstand, Joe would probably be away with some bird, as he would call her, who had been sitting in the front row, near the stage, eyeing him all night. He'd collect her and not be seen until it was time to play again. 'Look sharp, get the birds': that's a kind of West Indian thing! And he was always a very sharp dresser. He was slim, with well clipped beard, neatly trimmed hair and usually a narrow moustache and he would always wear well cut suits, white shirts and a collar and tie. He knew how to look impressive.

In deeper ways he always seemed a man apart. It was very difficult to have a conversation with him or even an argument. I found out very quickly that he would always state his position on whatever subject he wanted to talk about and that would be it. He had a very blinkered vision in that respect. I think that's how it was possible for him to imagine what he did and then carry it through – especially a couple of years or so after that first Frankfurt trip when his music was developing into something entirely new in jazz. There was a set pattern in the way his mind worked. If he had thought something over and got an idea and wanted to discuss it, you could not argue or debate about it with him. He would say what he thought and it would have to be accepted or else you'd do best to keep quiet or keep away from him. He was very self-centred. I did get to know him but somehow I never felt comfortable with him. Our minds never ran along the same lines, except about music.

Some of that was predictable given his background. He was born in 1928 in Jamaica and grew up as an orphan. He went to the Alpha School in Kingston, a school particularly for disadvantaged children and children with disabilities. It was founded as the Alpha Cottage School in 1880 and, run by Catholic nuns, it still exists today. It has always had a great reputation for fostering musical talent and giving the children there a sense of self-respect partly by developing their gifts for musical self-expression. The school gave some of those kids the chance to learn an instrument, whichever one they took to. Joe learned clarinet and joined the school orchestra. He started listening to classical music and studying it seriously and around the end of the 1940s jazz began to attract his attention. So, in a way, he started out in classical music as I had, but it must have been just what he could pick up in the school environment and our experiences were entirely different in every other way. The Alpha School catered for underprivileged children and Joe was certainly underprivileged. The fact that he was an orphan and had such a poor start in life accounts for what he became and his attitude towards other people.

You could say he lacked a kind of social warmth, an

ability to empathise with other people and get on with them. Because he had not been given that warmth as a child he could not produce it himself. He must have grown up longing to be appreciated for what he could do and, because he could play an instrument, he channelled all that longing through his music. You can hear it on the records. Sometimes his playing has a desperate cry. He's striving, almost fighting the music and dying to play it. He is saying through his music, 'I need a comeback from you'. He presents his strength to the world but he needs a return that says, 'We know you're strong but we love you.' On those rare occasions when he was really relaxed, when he didn't feel the need to show his hard side, it was absolutely wonderful, so lyrical. You can hear that on some of the records too, especially on one or two slow numbers.

At some point he got very involved with a religious sect called the Rosicrucians. They had enormous influence over him and that reinforced his single-mindedness. He absorbed a kind of self-preservation idea. From the time he was young he must have sensed he had to take care of himself because no-one else would do it. Somehow, that awareness, which was necessary to him, got exaggerated, so he never thought beyond 'I' and 'me'. The Rosicrucians taught him to think that way but he must have had it in him long before. It became pushed to a further extreme. So his concentration on the self meant that he always seemed remote. Perhaps also he was self-conscious because except in music his education was fairly limited and so his attitude was, 'Don't come too close. Don't question me.' He put up a barrier. I was not the only person around him who felt these things. Other people generally found the same problem. Because of it, he wasn't the best person to promote his music and his image. He was a loner and that was really unfortunate.

***

When the Joe Harriott Quintet was new and we were all enjoying developing the music, these things didn't matter too much to the group. We had steady work and were able to play the style of jazz we wanted. Apart from the Marquee on Saturday nights there was a regular gig on Sunday afternoons at the Flamingo, a jazz club which a young promoter named Jeff Kruger had been running since 1952, initially in a large room under the Mapleton Restaurant on the corner of Coventry Street and Wardour Street. As well as all that, I did other gigs, especially with Alan Clare. In fact, the Star Club, where I worked around this time with Alan, was a kind of offshoot of the Flamingo, managed by one of Jeff Kruger's associates.

Perhaps it was all too good to be true for our new quintet. Joe was never particularly healthy and on August 25th 1958, after the band had been in existence for five months, he suddenly collapsed and had to be rushed to hospital. It turned out to be pleurisy and pneumonia and he was out of action for several months. That was the beginning of various lung illnesses that recurred over the years. He never really looked after his health at all. He didn't eat properly and drank a lot. And you would never see him without a cigarette. When he was playing he would usually lodge his cigarette on some part of his saxophone so he could pick it up as soon as his solo was finished.

The collapse was serious. He went away from London to the countryside to recuperate at Pinewood Sanatorium and I visited him there. He spent some of his time writing pieces for the band, including the rocking, Basie-style blues 'Count Twelve' which became a favourite in the book. According to some accounts, at that time he also wrote an elaborate 'Pinewood Suite' which he planned to record but I don't remember us ever playing it and I know nothing about it. During his absence I looked after the band and we brought in the baritone sax player Harry Klein to take Joe's place for some gigs.

Five days after Joe had been rushed to hospital the infamous race riots occurred in Notting Hill, where I was living, then as now. Things had been building up and something or other had to happen I suppose. There was a lot of discontent amongst the black population in the area which, of course, had grown very much more numerous since the time Gertrude and I first moved there. I don't know what sparked it all but the police were very active and there was a restaurant, the Mangrove, where a lot of the agitation centred. It was all pretty depressing. A riot can't be anything else. It is the lowest you can get when people start fighting and killing each other. It was the beginning of the heavy drugs era and people started to make a lot of money out of that. Drugs situations always go from bad to worse.

But the rioting wasn't around the area where we lived and very fortunately we missed the whole thing. Gertrude and I had gone to Devon over those few days to see a former neighbour and while we were away two of our friends, visiting London, were living in our house and looking after it for us. We heard the news of the riots and asked about it all when we got back. The reply was a puzzled 'What riots?'. The people at our house didn't know anything about what had been happening. There had not been any sign of the rioting in our area at all and they hadn't listened to the news. But those events made national headlines and went down as one of the worst episodes for race relations in Britain.

Eventually, around the beginning of 1959, Joe came back from convalescence and then, in the spring, the quintet went abroad again. We had been invited to play at the San Remo Jazz Festival in Italy and as usual I travelled there by car. By then, of course, getting all over Europe on my own was a matter of familiar routine. On the way I would just turn up somewhere and book in for a night stop. And I'd always take my bass carefully into the hotel room or wherever I was. There was a lot of carrying to be done but I was always fit. In France there were Routiers to stay at, places used by lorry drivers and commercial travellers, and I'd have a list of Routiers and seek them out whenever I was in France.

So I drove to San Remo. Our spot was on the first day of the festival, Saturday February 21st, and it went well. The publicity had Joe billed as playing 'saxo contralto'. San Remo was the first festival we had played and there were many good European bands on the programme: the French tenor player Barney Wilen with his quintet; baritonist Lars Gullin; the Swiss altoist Flavio Ambrosetti; the trio of Barcelona pianist Tete Montoliu; and the brilliant German trombonist Albert Mangelsdorff with his group.

A couple of big American stars were on the bill, too. Sonny Rollins appeared with his trio of Henry Grimes on bass and drummer Peter Sims (later known as Pete La Roca). And Horace Silver's new quintet was there, with its powerhouse front line of trumpeter Blue Mitchell and tenorist Junior Cook which would stay together until Horace disbanded five years later. We had been using some of Horace's tunes in our repertoire and, with him in the audience listening, we made sure we included a couple of his things in our programme. He was really chuffed about that. He came up to Joe after our set and said, 'You make my tunes sound good! Look, I've got a lot of stuff, compositions and arrangements. I'll send you some when I get back to the States.' He was as good as his word and we took to playing quite a lot of his material after that.

Sonny Rollins' set was memorable for all the wrong reasons. Something upset him badly. He became unhappy with Henry Grimes' playing and was extremely rude to him, on stage in front of everyone. I thought it was disgusting to

treat a fellow musician that way and humiliate him in public. I talked to Henry afterwards and the guy was nearly in
tears. Rollins went on from San Remo to play in Paris and
the same thing happened there at a concert. I saw it
because I stopped off in Paris on the way back to London.
Rollins is a wonderful musician but I took a dislike to him
because of that. That kind of behaviour on stage wasn't
merited at all: putting the guy down in front of everyone.
Henry was a good bass player with a fine track record,
working with people like Gerry Mulligan, Anita O'Day,
Benny Goodman, Lee Konitz and Monk. Later he moved
into free jazz, but eventually, in the late 1960s, he gave up
his musical career. In all fairness, Sonny Rollins must have
been going through a bad time then. Soon after, for a number of reasons, Rollins retired from playing publicly for two
years to reassess his life and his music. Eventually, of course,
he came back a stronger soloist than ever.

The festival was held over the two days of the weekend
and on the Saturday night there was a jam session with
some of the musicians from the festival at a plush restaurant in the hills above the town. That was where I had the
chance to play with Gullin and, as I said earlier, the conversations with him during those two days on the Italian
Riviera were a real pleasure, one of the most vivid memories from that trip.

Back in Britain, the quintet had the opportunity to make its
first records. We recorded four tracks on May 5th 1959 for
an EP which was issued under the title *Blue Harriott*.
Presumably it was called that because all the pieces were
blues-based in one way or another and, appropriately
enough, the dark, gloomy, blue-tinted cover photo featured
a depressed looking Joe, sitting on the edge of the piano
stool with his head resting in his hands, dangling the ever-
present smouldering cigarette. We made the record at the

Lansdowne Recording Studios in west London, owned by a flamboyant promoter and producer named Denis Preston.

Denis turned out to be a very good friend to Joe and the quintet. Ultimately, he was the only record producer who gave the band a chance and stayed with it as its style became much more challenging in later years. That makes him a cut above a lot of people in my eyes. Without him, the band's music probably would not have been recorded at all. Hardly anyone else showed any interest and all the quintet's records except the last one – which we did for the jazz record shop proprietor Doug Dobell – were made at the Lansdowne Studios for Denis.

I don't know how Joe first got involved with Preston but I remember that Denis had a black girlfriend and knew some of the black musicians in London. He was certainly a smart operator, a bit of a go-getter, and apparently did very well indeed in his business. He had set up the Lansdowne Studios in 1955 in what appeared, from the quiet leafy street in which it was situated, to be just an old, elegant, private apartment block.

The studios were an entirely independent operation and Denis recorded whatever he wanted and whatever he thought would sell, from calypso music and spoken word records to popular music, blues and traditional, mainstream and modern jazz. He would license out the tapes to record companies for release. So eventually there was a 'Lansdowne Jazz Series' issued by EMI on the Columbia label and in the United States some of the records came out on Jazzland. Some of Denis' records – such as Acker Bilk's huge success 'Stranger on the Shore' in 1961 – became popular hits, so that must have brought the money in for him. I didn't know him well and Joe did all the dealing with him but Denis obviously loved jazz and wanted to see it prosper. And his commitment to the quintet's music lasted long after he could have hoped to make any money from it.

From my point of view, the best thing about the Lansdowne Studios was the superb sound quality on the recordings we did there. Denis had excellent recording equipment including very good tape machines and the best microphones. And he used highly skilled recording staff who could accurately capture the sound of my amplified bass. Many recording engineers, over the years, couldn't do that properly and some could only manage it more or less on a trial and error basis. Often, at the end of a recording session, after endless experimenting by the engineer, the sound of the bass would finally be just about right. In fact, I can sometimes tell the order the tracks were recorded at a session by the gradual improvement in the sound of the bass and the balance of the instruments on the record. I can't remember who the engineer was for *Blue Harriott* but on later Lansdowne albums we recorded, such as *Free Form* and *Abstract*, it was Adrian Kerridge, and he did a fine job on the sound.

The studio itself was underground, so it was quiet, completely insulated from all the traffic noise around Holland Park. It wasn't huge but it was a comfortable size for relatively small groups. From the studio floor you had to climb steps to get to the control booth where the recording equipment was housed and from inside the booth you could look out through a big sound-proof window down to the recording floor below with all the microphones and wires.

The *Blue Harriott* date was the first occasion when I worked at Lansdowne but Denis had recorded Joe several times before. He had set up a date three years previously featuring Harriott with a string section in a similar way to the recordings of Charlie Parker with strings by Norman Granz in America for Verve. In fact, according to Jim Godbolt in his book about the history of jazz in Britain, Denis saw himself very much as the British Norman Granz.

We recorded 'Count Twelve', 'Still Goofin'' (a fast version

of the band's theme 'Just Goofin''), Harry South's 'Jumpin' With Joe' and Horace Silver's 'Señor Blues', all of which were standard items in the group's repertoire by that time. On the record, the ensemble themes shout out on all four numbers, as though the band is bursting with enthusiasm, and everyone gets solo space. I play bowed and hummed solos on the medium-tempo 'Count Twelve' and the faster 'Jumpin' With Joe', and a plucked solo on 'Still Goofin''.

It's interesting to compare those recordings – the only ones with that particular personnel that were issued commercially – with an acetate I have of a recording for a BBC 'Jazz Club' broadcast three months later. Maybe we had been slightly nervous going into the studio for the first time as a group for the *Blue Harriott* date. Certainly, the performances we did on August 13th for the 'Jazz Club' broadcast sound more relaxed and the quintet sounds looser, more willing to take risks in performance and bursting with ideas. Along with 'Count Twelve' and 'Señor Blues' there are versions of two of the other Horace Silver tunes in our book, 'Buhaina' – a great bop line – and the medium-up tempo 'The Outlaw', featuring a passionate solo by Joe and Harry's rolling piano style. With Hank sitting out, Joe also plays a ballad feature, a lovely version of 'Autumn in New York'. On the tape the presenter interviews Joe briefly about the group's San Remo trip and the Horace Silver connection and Joe reveals that Horace sent over no less than 18 arrangements, though I'm sure we didn't use all of them.

Joe had very fixed ideas about how the bass should sound. He didn't like amplification on it, although he accepted that the amplified instrument was what I played and he went along with that. But he didn't approve of my bowing and humming style and on later records with the quintet I didn't include it and usually plucked my solos, although I used the bow frequently on some of the free form pieces. I don't remember us seriously discussing any of those matters of style. As I said, you couldn't discuss things with Joe. But we were all experienced musicians and knew how to fit in with what the group sound seemed to need for whatever piece we were playing.

Another striking instance of Joe's single-minded way of doing things arose when we went back to the Storyville Club for a further three week engagement in October 1959. What particularly sticks in my memory is something that came up on the car journey to Frankfurt. On that occasion, for some reason, Joe travelled as a passenger in my car rather than making his own way to Germany. We didn't talk a lot on the way: there was never much small talk with him. But at some point he decided to start telling me about some musical ideas he had been mulling over.

As we drove along, he began to set them out in his usual very forthright way. I don't know how these thoughts had first arisen, but he had started to imagine that there might be a way of playing jazz that didn't require harmonies fixed in advance, chord sequences, which the music had always relied on as a basis for improvisation up to that time. He said he thought it could be possible to play without those pre-determined harmonies and, in fact, without any pre-conceptions at all about what was to be played and how. The idea would be to rely on complete spontaneity from all the musicians: to let the group's free interaction create har-monies and musical relationships between the instruments that had not been planned in advance.

So we spent a lot of time in the car talking about this idea of there being no harmony, no harmonic structures, what the implications would be for a group that tried to play that way and how it could be made to work musically. From my point of view, of course, I wanted to know what he thought I would do in this new music, what my role would be and what I would play. And his reply to all those questions was,

'Well, you could play diminished series, diminished runs.' A diminished run is a sequence of notes that follow each other in exact intervals, so the sequence is bound to contain a note that will harmonise at the right moment. You don't need chords to guarantee *some* kind of harmony. Some notes will fit harmonically as the bass backs the soloist's melodic line. If you continuously play diminished runs you'll always hit the right notes somewhere, but to me that sounded very dull and uninteresting.

I thought, 'My God, does that mean I'm going to spend my whole time playing those runs over and over? I'm supposed to produce nothing but diminished runs for however long he's playing?' That seemed the most boring thing possible and I couldn't visualise doing it at all, playing in an utterly repetitious, mechanical way. Of course, later, once we actually started to have a go at playing what eventually came to be known as free form music, I began to hear what was possible and did what came to me, what I thought was the right approach. There turned out to be a lot of possibilities. It certainly wasn't a matter of playing diminished runs.

But in the car I started to think: 'Well, if he wants to do this and that is the role he thinks I am going to play in it, I'll really have to study this and come up with something better. I'll have to convince him there are other ways to try to achieve what he wants.' The point is that he was only thinking about what he wanted to produce and not thinking at all about what the other guys might do. That was how Joe was. He never thought about the other guys. The only thing was the music and how he wanted it to be. In that context it's interesting that I don't remember him ever using my name. He didn't address me or the others personally. When we rehearsed or recorded he would tend to say something like, 'The bass can play four bars here', or 'The bass will have to lead in to the theme statement there.' It was quite impersonal really.

He never had much sense of humour but he would often say things unintentionally in a funny way as though his mind was on another plane from the person he was talking to and he was making connections in his thoughts that would be very odd to anyone else. Michael Garrick, the pianist and composer with whom Joe and I worked a great deal in later years, has a whole stock of Harriott expressions. According to Joe, when he and Dizzy Gillespie first played together, 'after a couple of numbers we were like *swallows on d'water*'. Michael wrote and recorded a composition called 'Swallows on the Water', dedicated to Harriott. On another occasion, according to Michael, Joe declared: 'All the others, they play *inside*, *here* in d'room. But what *I* play is out d'window, *out* d'window.' Michael exaggerates the West Indian accent a bit because Joe tended to talk in a formal and stilted, rather than lilting way. He often sounded stiff and unbending. He wasn't someone who could laugh at himself, but there were some funny moments. After we had played a gig at a jazz in club in Manchester, I packed up my gear and went looking for Harriott, who had disappeared. Outside in the street a brawl was going on between two women and Joe was standing by, unconcerned, taking the occasional drag on his cigarette. 'Oh, don't worry, man,' he said. 'They're just fighting over me.'

His life style was totally different from mine. He lived in a flat in west London near Maida Vale. If you needed to contact him during the day you always knew where he would be: in the betting shop. Gambling on horses was one of his addictions, along with the smoking and booze. And there was a club in Old Compton Street, the Downbeat, where a lot of musicians would go because there was always good music. We would sometimes relax there after playing and Joe practically lived on the fruit machine at the Downbeat. He loved gambling. But I never remember him using any hard drugs. And alongside all the mundane, pointless, everyday life, he spent a lot of time thinking deeply about connections between fine art and music and working out his artistic ideas on some abstract plane, even if, as Val Wilmer wrote from a journalist's perspective after she interviewed him, he 'had a tendency to leave questions unanswered, to make statements that sounded impressive but didn't quite add up in the end.'

As far as I know, he never had any real family life, which made his situation completely different from mine. At one time there was a stable relationship with a young woman who did some kind of political work. Joe was close to her but I think she was the only woman who was really a part of his life. All the others he met on tours or just incidentally. It must have been a lonely life and, of course, that is not a way of satisfying the need to be loved.

In November 1959 he had a major engagement without the band. He was invited, together with the baritone saxist Ronnie Ross, to play alongside the Modern Jazz Quartet on their British tour that month. As far as the quintet was concerned, the regular gigs continued, mainly at the Marquee. Then, early in 1960, Harriott fell ill again. The lung troubles had come back. He was in hospital for about five weeks and during that time he wrote some of the compositions that, months later, we started to use as vehicles for the free form jazz idea he had begun to explain to me on the second Frankfurt trip.

Joe's increasingly enthusiastic talk about free form soon produced serious tensions in the band. Hank Shaw and Harry South were not interested at all. The new approach Joe was trying to get us to adopt involved drawing on all the musical resources each of us had. If you're being asked to play without any preconceptions it follows that you must have a lot of musical knowledge that can be brought into play at any time as the music dictates. Hank, being self-taught, had equipped himself to work in a particular idiom he loved – bebop. He didn't want to stray from that and he couldn't see the point. Hank was much more of an out-and-out bop man than Harry but both of them were dead against free form and wouldn't co-operate, so there was no point in carrying on with the idea as long as they were in the band.

The quintet rehearsed fairly regularly, maybe once a fortnight, at Dinely's Rehearsal Rooms off Marylebone High Street. One day, Joe brought some of his free form compositions along to the rehearsal. After the theme, which he had written out fully, there were no guides, no chord sequences to play, nothing. The idea was to try to see where our collective imagination would lead the piece. He would put these compositions in front of us all and say, 'You play this to start with and then we'll see what happens.' And, of course, nothing would happen because Hank's and Harry's hearts weren't in it.

Once I had decided that I definitely would not play diminished runs but that there might be other possibilities, I began to develop some enthusiasm at least to try what Joe had in mind. I thought it could be exciting and I wanted to discover how it might work out because I saw that it would give us the chance to be as creative and imaginative musically as we could be and I would have the chance to draw on all my musical training.

But it wasn't possible to play free form unless everyone in the group was sympathetic and thinking along the same lines. So Joe gave up with it as far as the existing quintet was concerned. The experiments were confined to Dinely's and never reached the ears of the public at the Marquee or anywhere else.

In April 1960 we went back to the Lansdowne Studios to make another EP. There was no hint of Joe's free form ideas in the pieces recorded. On the 8th we did a version of 'Caravan', with Frank Holder added on bongo drums. Frank is a very good percussionist and singer, a great showman and a cabaret artiste in his own right. He often used to sit in with the quintet at the Marquee around that time and, in fact, he had come with us for the second Storyville Club engagement in Frankfurt. He made nice sounds and varieties of rhythm and fitted in well. In fact, he would record with the quintet once more, a year or so later. Meanwhile, on April 21st, the group completed the new EP with performances (without Frank) of 'Liggin'', 'Southern Horizons', 'Tuesday Morning Swing' and 'You Go To My Head': all well-established items in the quintet's book, things we played regularly at the Marquee at that time.

But, in fact, a very significant change in the personnel had already occurred before those sessions. Hank Shaw, no doubt seeing which way the wind was blowing with the group, left in early February, soon after Joe had started to bring his new free form compositions along to rehearsals. His replacement from mid-March was a West Indian trumpeter named Shake Keane. Shake originally came from St. Vincent but had been in London for some years. I had known him for a long time and recommended him to Joe because I was aware that he was an excellent musician and I thought he would be sympathetic to the directions we wanted to follow with the band.

So the April recording sessions took place with Shake on trumpet in place of Hank. Then, in early May, Harry South left. I knew exactly who we needed to replace him. Alan Clare had a pianist friend in Edinburgh, who had been practising as a solicitor there and was uncertain about making the break from a legal career and moving to London to become a full-time musician. His name was Pat Smythe. He used to send tapes down from Scotland for Alan to hear and when Alan played them to me at the Studio Club I was very impressed indeed. Later, when Pat came to London I had the chance to play with him. I loved his playing from the beginning. He had a harmonic subtlety and a range and depth of musical knowledge that was out of the ordinary. So I persuaded Joe to take him on and suddenly we had a rather different quintet from the hard bop band that had been formed two years earlier. Trying out Harriott's free form ideas suddenly became a real possibility again.

8.

free form

By May 1960, the Harriott Quintet had an almost entirely new personnel. Joe and I were the only survivors from the original band. Harry South and Hank Shaw had gone, and at that time Bobby Orr decided to leave too and was replaced by Tommy Jones, who kept us going for five months until Phil Seamen was available to join in November.

Apart from regular work at the Marquee on Saturdays and the Flamingo on Sundays, the quintet played various festivals. In late May we appeared at the Bath Festival and the BBC arranged an outside broadcast. Then in August there was the Beaulieu Jazz Festival, a rain-drenched affair that year. During the summer we continued to play the quintet's standard repertoire in public appearances but in rehearsals we were working hard on Joe's new ideas about free form and, with the new personnel, we soon made a lot of headway. The group gelled and instead of fighting Joe's radical plans everyone began to contribute to them and each of us tried to work out in terms of our own playing how to turn them into practice. It was an exciting time because we felt we were breaking new ground.

Amongst ourselves we didn't discuss the theory of what we were doing very much. Joe would say something like, 'What we are about to do is to try to paint a picture in colour.' He often liked to draw analogies with painting. The sounds of the music were like colours in an abstract painting. He meant that we would use different sounds to express a mood or feeling, to paint abstract pictures in sound. It was a good analogy. Those of us who had had a bit of classical training could see what he had in mind. Shake Keane, Pat Smythe and myself had had experience of classical music and we could understand that idea of using music impressionistically and creating some kind of overall texture of sound in which each instrument is just a component. When we started there were many things happening that were not right in the music but we gradually found ways we could operate to make good sounds, to make something come out of it, developing a whole performance with complete spontaneity.

In rehearsing, the first thing was always to learn the theme of the piece thoroughly. Joe's themes were always very detailed and intricate so they suggested a lot of ideas that could be developed in improvisation. Usually the idea was for the theme to open and close the performance of the piece and what happened in between the opening and closing theme statements would be completely spontaneous improvisation with no set tempo or rhythms or harmonic structure. Any of those things could vary between different performances of the same composition. Sometimes the performance would be marvellous and at other times it wouldn't quite gel.

Joe always brought his compositions to rehearsal with a title given to them. So, in playing, we would try to paint a picture of whatever ideas the title conjured up, whatever we thought Joe had imagined in connection with the theme he had written. He had had the vision first, which he had tried to express through his composition, and our job in the group was to imagine what it was he wanted from the performance of that piece. It needed a lot of imagination and we had no models to follow. But we discovered that it could work when we all shared the same ideas about the way we were trying to make music.

The titles of Harriott's free form pieces are always short, usually single words, and they seem cryptic and opaque at first but they all have meaning and are very important. As a player you could find the meaning in them. Some pieces eventually recorded on the quintet's *Abstract* album are good examples. 'Subject' was a very short theme before we started to develop it. From those few notes you just had to let your imagination go and try to produce *brown* sounds. 'Shadows' was the most potent of all for me: something eerie, obviously to do with darkness and mystery, dark colours. The phrasing had to produce the mysterious element, and rhythmic movements would suggest flitting about in the shadows trying to locate something. It's entirely an exercise of imagination. I loved that piece because it encouraged us to be very adventurous and gave me the chance to play everything I could. 'Compound', which is almost completely given over to a duet between jazz drums and bongo drums, is a compound of dense, shifting rhythms. So the titles set our minds working in certain directions. That was the whole idea.

How do you play bass in free form music? Well, very fortunately, if I hear a phrase or a tone in my head I can always produce it on the instrument. That is why I can play my solos and sing along with them. I'm blessed that way. So where there is no set harmony in the music being played you have to be able, nevertheless, to *hear* a harmony that can relate to it. Where several notes are sounded you have to be able to find a harmonic connection between them and bring it out in your playing. When I hear notes played together there is always a harmony suggested to me. My job is to bring out the right harmony for that moment in the music. I found I could do that with the quintet, suggesting a harmonic root for whatever notes the other instruments were playing.

Having a piano in the group creates a further complication. It is necessary for bass and piano to be in very close empathy with each other because it would be easy to have disastrous clashes if the choices of harmonies between the instruments were different. A lot of free improvising groups can't function with a piano because the piano lays down harmonies in too definite and inflexible a way. But with Pat Smythe there was no problem. When we performed I was always positioned close to the piano and could hear every move he made in the music. And Pat had an acute ability to listen and respond. It was a very rare thing between us. We both listened very carefully to each other and functioned as a tight team. Whatever he heard in the music, I heard. We thought along the same lines, hearing and creating the same harmonies.

In the end, whatever elements of style you are bringing in, whatever idioms you are drawing on, it's just *music*. It is like a musical envelope that can include all kinds of things, depending on the needs of the performance and the details that go into it. We more or less managed to stay in the envelope together! Of course, making music in that intuitive way is risky. It takes a great deal of concentration. In theory, you can hit wrong notes and everything could clash and become chaotic. But, in practice, I felt that that rarely happened in the quintet once we had learned enough about each other's musical thinking. You could avoid clashes by reacting quickly. If I hit a note that I found was wrong I would quickly move to a right one and play it in such a way that the 'wrong' note would become a passing note. The passing note is not strictly on the scale, but it leads in to the right one, so it can sound right itself.

I loved playing with Pat. He was my favourite pianist. I had a great understanding of what he was about and I think he had the same feeling about me. He was very quietly spoken and perhaps a little reserved in a nice way – a pleasant person, earnest and quite a deep thinker. It took him a long time to decide definitely to follow a musical career and he was 37 when he joined the quintet, which was his first major job as a professional musician. He had a false start. He had previously moved from his native city, Edinburgh, to London for a time in 1958 and worked with Dizzy Reece's quartet. But then he went back to Scotland to finish his law studies and become a solicitor. Alan Clare always used to rave to me about Pat's playing while Pat was still living in Edinburgh and occasionally Pat would come to London to see Alan. When he finally made the permanent move to London and a chance came to get him into the Harriott Quintet I knew it would make a huge difference to have him with us.

The first great thing about his playing was his sensitive, subtle touch. With Harriott he found ways of accompanying that never hampered the freedom of the front line players but could add an amazing range of textures and colours in sound. He played a wide range of music, classically-inspired things and so on. And his fluency of phrasing was outstanding. Basically, he just had a completely different approach from most of the piano players I had heard at the time. It struck me that his musical knowledge and background was very sound and I always loved hearing him play, whatever the context. I don't know exactly what his background in classical music was, but he must have had that training. He couldn't have learned what he knew just by tinkling on the keys.

While Pat and I developed into a tight team in the rhythm section, the partnership of Shake Keane and Joe made a near-perfect front line. Shake's style was very much his own: lyrical, expressive and powerful. When you hear it now on the records it's unusual: earthy and at the same time ethereal, a wonderful mixture, very imaginative with plenty of humour. Some people think he was the finest trumpeter who ever played in this country. *Grove's Dictionary of Jazz* says that his playing 'always retained a singing, shapely sense of melody and he soon became recognised as the most accomplished jazz trumpeter of his generation in England.' I think that's right. To me, he was certainly the finest flugelhorn player we have had. His sound stood out a mile from all the others. In fact, he had a lot of difficulty getting that sound. He started using a trumpet mouthpiece on the flugelhorn because he had trouble with flugelhorn mouthpieces. Eventually he had one specially made but he always had problems getting the right mouthpiece for the sound he wanted.

The musical closeness of Joe and Shake in the quintet was easy to see right from the beginning when we rehearsed free form pieces. We would play the main theme together to get it right. And when we'd done that so that we had it perfect, we would start to see how we could develop it. After the theme statement it would often be Shake who would take off first, starting to improvise, because he was always very adventurous and imaginative, full of ideas and all ready to go. Then Joe would catch on to something Shake had played. Meanwhile, hearing these two together would spark us in the rhythm section into doing something appropriate. A lot depended on the trumpet and the alto, what direction they would take. That would set us on a suitable path. In the rhythm section we took our lead from the front line but Pat and I might sometimes have to create the lead if that was what the piece required.

When we played free form no-one decided on an order of solos. It wasn't a question of solos at all. It was just a matter of who would lead off with a phrase to set the direction. That opening phrase would spark ideas in the rest of the group so that the ideas could grow into something we would develop collectively. Shake would start something or Joe might start and then Shake would hear a phrase that inspired him. Sometimes they would play in turn for a few bars, and sometimes their lines would soar and tumble together, intertwined. We never talked about who would take the lead at any particular time in any given piece. But in rehearsals Joe might lead off because he knew what he wanted and needed to show us.

On the records there is usually no hint of hesitation about who's going to come forward after the theme statement so it might sound to the listener as though it's been worked out. But it just happened. Of course, you can hear that often the trumpet and alto *are* playing together, darting in and out, chasing each other, vying with each other to get their ideas out into the mix that made up the whole group performance. Shake and Joe made a great team. As Val Wilmer wrote, Shake was the musical partner Joe had waited for all along.

His full name was Ellsworth McGranahan Keane but he got his nickname (short for Shakespeare) early in life, because of his love of literature. Over the years he gained a big reputation as a Caribbean poet, and many volumes of his writings have been published. He studied and played music and worked as a teacher in St. Vincent before he came to Britain to study English literature in the early 1950s. After that, putting his formal literary studies on hold, he immersed himself in the music scene. He recorded calypsos with singer Lord Kitchener and West African highlife music with pianist Mike McKenzie, and played with many jazz bands around the London clubs. He was 32 when he joined Harriott.

The first time I had heard him play was in a Mayfair nightclub. Then, later, sometime during the 1950s, the opportunity arose for me to work on Sundays for a time in a quintet. The leader, a pianist named Harry White, hired top musicians so it was a real joy to play with them. Among them was Shake and from that time I began to appreciate how good he was. He played mostly trumpet then but also very occasionally flugelhorn and it was the flugel that really got to me. He was unsure about the instrument but I persuaded him to keep on playing it, which he did more and more. Thank goodness! Because he had a sound and feeling on the flugel that nobody else had. With the quintet, and on records under his own name, he played it a lot.

Shake was larger than life. Physically he was huge and had a wonderful, deep, resonant voice. Being a student of literature and a writer himself, his command of English was always good and, often, when he was in a certain mood, he would delight in speaking philosophically and eloquently about music, politics or anything that had captured his interest. He loved to talk, holding forth in those mellow tones. I often heard him recite some of his poems when, in later years, we were both involved with poetry and jazz concerts. His character was a strange mix: strong and weak. He had a powerful personality in some ways but he lacked self-control when he had had too much to drink.

When you allowed for his foibles and saw him as a whole man, he was a lovely person and when you got to know him he was very warm-hearted. He would throw his arms around you in a great bearhug and, being such a big chap, almost engulf you. I felt an affinity with him straight away. For a start, our Caribbean backgrounds drew us close together and we felt the same way about a lot of things. We always got on wonderfully. In fact, he was my best friend.

Eventually he came to live in my house, on the ground floor, with his family.

The ladies all loved him but unfortunately he did not make a success of his marriage. I think perhaps the difference in background and outlook between him and his wife was too great. He knew what he wanted, he was very strong-minded, and I suppose he didn't always achieve it and often felt frustrated. But although he lived in such close proximity to me and I cared about him, I wouldn't interfere in those sort of personal relationships at all. That was something he had to solve between himself and his wife. Gertrude and I got on very well with her and we're still great friends. But they just didn't hit it off together some-how. It was sad. And they had two nice boys.

In November 1960, there was another important change of personnel in the quintet. In a way, at the time, it seemed like putting the last piece in the musical jigsaw, the last ele-ment needed to make Joe's perfect band. Phil Seamen replaced Tommy Jones on drums. Now we had maybe the best jazz drummer in Britain to complete our group. Phil had worked with Tubby Hayes' quartet just before he joined Harriott, and before that with Don Rendell, the Jazz Couriers, Dizzy Reece and any number of other top bands. He was a big jazz star and a driving, authoritative drummer.

Phil's sense of time was his great asset. He had a terrific technique and imagination so that he could always play the right thing at the right time. He and I worked very, very well together: no complications there. But throughout the time he was with the quintet he was often in a terrible state physically. He had been a heroin addict for a long time. As his condition worsened over the years he deteriorated phys-ically and would get extremely tired. It would be very diffi-cult for him to keep a good steady tempo if we were playing an uptempo thing but his natural ability was such that when he was feeling awful he could still play great stuff. He was a natural. It's a great shame he mistreated himself so much.

In the months before Phil joined, we had started to experiment with free form at the Marquee. Bob Dawbarn wrote in *Melody Maker* in September in slightly bewildered tones: 'Some decidedly odd sounds have been issuing from London's Marquee Club recently. Patient tracking will reveal the Joe Harriott Quintet rehearsing what Joe claims to be something completely new in jazz... Harriott is on the track of something new... it may well prove important to the development of British jazz.' Now the news was out that we were trying to do something strange and different – and when we started to introduce free form into the sets at the Marquee the band instantly became the most controversial group on the London jazz scene.

Joe tried to explain what we were doing in interviews in the musical press: 'The soloist dominates what is going on but there may be moments when the rhythm section dominates and suggests a new idea. The soloist plays for just as long as he wants to and then makes way for the next man. We are not playing in choruses and are not even bound by bar lines, so he can stop whenever he likes.' But talking about solos was just a way of explaining to people used to orthodox jazz ideas. Really the whole group was creating together, and different members took the lead and were prominent at different times in the performance. Pat Smythe tried to explain ideas about harmony that we were using: in ordinary jazz 'the chords come off that conveyor belt – big ones, small ones and so on – and you are dominated by them. In our new music you can play the normal changes if you want to, but there is somehow more reason for it if you do.' We didn't feel we had to lean on chord sequences like a crutch. We could use a wider range of musical ideas. How do you avoid dischords? 'You have to concentrate the whole time. If it clashes – well, that's part it.' Now, forty years later, these ideas are commonplace in jazz. But then they were absolutely revolutionary. No-one else in Britain was thinking along those lines and what we were trying to do as a group was unlike anything going on in jazz anywhere in the world at that time.

My diary has an entry pencilled in for September 2nd 1960: 'Audition. Denis Preston'. No doubt Denis wanted to hear the quintet's new music in studio conditions to check it out properly before he agreed to set up a date to record it. The diary page also notes that we played the Flamingo Club in Wardour Street that evening. Then, nearly two months later, we went to the Lansdowne Studios to make *Free Form*, the first full LP the quintet had recorded and its first recordings of free form jazz, or what Joe sometimes called 'abstract music'. I don't have a note of the dates of the recording sessions, but Tony Middleton's Harriott discography lists them as Wednesday November 23rd and Wednesday November 30th. Certainly there would have been two sessions, because we recorded a lot of music.

The *Free Form* album came out on the Jazzland label. Listening to it you can hear the new ideas we were trying to bring into the music at that time. The themes are intended to throw out ideas for improvisation by the whole group. Often the tempo varies dramatically in a composition. 'Abstract' has a fast, furious line for the horns that gives way suddenly to slow chords. Then the improvisation that follows is very fast with Shake starting out, Joe commenting and the two horns chasing each other with a stinging cymbal rhythm driving everything along. The theme of 'Formation' has bright fanfares and long sequences of agitated single notes. After it has been played, alto and trumpet vie for the lead but the alto quickly dominates and the trumpet gives way. After a short alto solo the trumpet returns to make its statement and matters are resolved in a loose duet between the horns that leads to a relaxed chordal piano solo. 'Coda', lasting almost eight minutes – the longest piece on the album, has the fast lines of its theme played by the horns over an ambling, easy rhythm. Then all the instruments interact in different combinations, with Pat first taking the lead and Joe setting up trills behind. On 'Parallel' the theme mixes song-like phrases, dramatic rising arpeggios and cascades of notes. In this piece, the piano improvisation with bass backing illustrates how close Pat and I were musically, picking up each other's phrases and completing each other's voicings. 'Calypso Sketches' is another contrast. A light, uncomplicated tune leads to relaxed improvising by Joe over a lilting rhythm.

On these recordings the improvised parts don't seem like solos. There are always passages where one instrument is clearly out in front, but they rarely last long or end with one instrument stopping and another beginning. More usually, one instrument begins to comment on another's melodic line, breaking in and setting up a countermelody or a rhythmic idea. Then that instrument takes over for a time. But everyone contributes to the direction of the piece and any member of the group could lead the music at any time. Because there were no fixed choruses you couldn't arrange for each player to solo for a certain number of choruses and so control the length of a performance that way. But performances had to be limited to fit on the record so if it seemed that a piece might go on too long the supervisor in the recording booth would switch on a red light in the studio and then we would bring the music gradually back to the final theme and take it out.

The last piece we were scheduled to perform for the album was the fierce 'Tempo', which is played very fast on the recording. Its six minutes include wild, exhilarating interplay between alto and trumpet. But you can hear on this track that Phil Seamen is exhausted and – ironically, given the title – struggling to keep the tempo. He switches to brushes at one point and then back to sticks. He takes a solo towards the end of the piece, but it is very subdued. I remember that Phil could barely finish that last number. He was getting slower, as you can hear in places on the record, but he just made it. In the final theme statement he managed the aggressive accenting with all his usual force and precision. He could usually find that last ounce of energy from somewhere to give to the music. He never played badly. But he was really finished after that. He couldn't have played any more that day at anything like that tempo.

It wasn't possible to depend on Phil in the way that Bobby Orr could always be depended on. Bobby always kept perfect tempo. With some drummers, once a piece begins they're off and the tempo races away or slows down but with Bobby the beat was always there and you knew exactly where it was. Yet Phil always had the ideas. Bobby provided a solid background to work on, always so correct, but perhaps not as imaginative as Phil. Phil would surprise you more. He had some special inspiration that often made his playing very exciting indeed. But you need to have a steadiness in the tempos. During the period he worked with the quintet Phil gradually found it harder to keep that steadiness.

Something strange happened after we had finished recording 'Tempo'. It's become a bit of a legend that another, totally unscheduled piece was also recorded at the Lansdowne Studios late that day, despite Phil's exhaustion. What happened was that we were all starting to pack our instruments up to go home. Phil was getting ready to dismantle his kit and Pat Smythe was still at the piano. He was doodling something or other on the keys and Seamen picked up his cowbell and pinged it, maybe accidentally at first. It happened to be pitched in A and Pat immediately went into playing in the key of the cowbell. While that was happening, Shake was walking around the studio relaxing a bit. He had a glass in his hand from which he was drinking brandy. When Phil sounded the cowbell, Shake hit the tumbler with a pencil he was holding and – would you believe it? – that tumbler was just in pitch with the cowbell.

When I heard that, immediately I got the feeling that we could play something. So I called to the recording engineer, 'Run the tape, run the tape. We've got something here. We're going to play something.' Pat started to play the phrases he had been trying before and then I came in. No-one knew what we were going to play. We started to create something around the tone of the cowbell and the tumbler. Pat produced a dreamy modal piano improvisation and Joe, who had been up in the control box ready to listen to a play-back, saw what was happening and picked up his alto and came down the stairs to join us, adding quiet flurries of notes behind the piano chords. Then Shake joined in, building the tension, so that finally the whole group was improvising together.

Nothing had been planned. Everything happened because of the cowbell and the tumbler. But that performance on tape became 'Modal'. There wasn't room for it on the *Free Form* album, which was already 45 minutes long – a good length for an LP in those days. So it was held back and eventually included on the quintet's second album, *Abstract*. Many years later, long after Shake had moved away from London, he would return to visit me and every time he came he wanted to hear 'Modal', this slow, pretty piece which nobody composed or even intended and which just happened at that moment. We thought about this so much. The ironic thing is that it was credited to Harriott like all the other pieces on the record. But he had nothing to do with the start of it at all.

***

It was almost exactly a year – November 22nd 1961 – before we went back to the Lansdowne Studios to record more free form music. The pieces we did on that occasion show that Joe had found ways to structure free performances so that none of the spontaneity in the music was lost but more variety of form could be introduced in individual pieces. 'Pictures' required the horns and the rhythm section to alternate, never actually meeting up until the end of the performance. 'Idioms' presented several themes, carried by different instruments. Joe had invited Frank Holder along to the session and the exciting 'Compound', with its powerful shifting rhythms, features him on conga and bongos in a dazzling virtuoso duet with Phil Seamen. Only right at the end of the piece does the rest of the group come in with the final theme statement.

When we returned to Lansdowne several months later to complete what would become the *Abstract* album, Phil Seamen wasn't with us. Things couldn't really continue with him in the band. Phil and I had got on reasonably well at a personal level. He'd have his funny quips, his cockney humour. But, despite all his brilliance as a musician, he became a liability for the quintet. He was so heavily into dope and stuff that, as time went on, he was too unreliable. On a couple of occasions we had to start gigs without him and at many other times we would be hanging around waiting, not knowing what kind of state he would be in when he appeared.

One of the worst occasions was a concert at the Hammersmith Odeon in west London. The Dave Brubeck Quartet was booked to play and we were the support group. What happened was a nightmare. We were supposed to play the first half and it came time to start. Brubeck was standing in the wings. But there was no Phil. So we had to go on stage without him. We began the first number and then suddenly he came rushing onstage from somewhere and got behind the drums. And there and then, in front of everybody, he was sick all over the place with Brubeck standing watching us. Aaagh! At that point I wished the stage would open up and swallow us. It was so awful, so horrible.

We just had to keep on playing. The concert had started so we had to go on. I don't know whether the incident was reported in the musical press. We couldn't have avoided that unless perhaps, as Phil was at the back of the stage, people at the front in the theatre did not realise what was happening. Anyway, Phil just got on with playing. I suppose to him it was a normal occurrence. That that was the way he was. When he played it was wonderful but the rest of it – terrible. Finally everyone was fed up. In the spring of 1962 Bobby Orr came back to replace him in the group and it was Bobby who played on the final session for the *Abstract* album.

One good thing came out of that Hammersmith concert. I met Gene Wright, Brubeck's bass player. With Brubeck himself it was just a matter of hello and a handshake. But Gene was very friendly and came to my house, though it was a fleeting visit as Brubeck's quartet was travelling on tour and he didn't have much time. He really took to my bass. He wanted to buy it but, of course, I wasn't selling.

Gradually we stepped up the amount of free form in the sets we played at the Marquee and elsewhere. Joe told the press around that time that our new music was 'being given a fair hearing and a fair reception... I know this music has no obvious commercial appeal, but I think in the next five years, maybe longer, it will take over, become the thing. There are pointers that way.'

By then, of course, there were some clear pointers coming from America. Ornette Coleman's music was the main thing, but after we first heard it we always felt that what he was doing was entirely different from what we had been attempting. No one knows when Joe first had the idea of free form but Pat Smythe told Roger Cotterrell in a phone conversation in the early 1970s that Harriott had been trying out free form in rehearsals with Dizzy Reece as early as 1958. I know nothing about that and Pat is no longer alive to add to what he said but certainly it was much later before we in the quintet first heard any of Ornette's music. In any case I don't think there was any connection between what Ornette did and what we were doing because his music then was strictly a solo effort. It was a soloist playing free, not a group playing free. You can imagine a soloist playing free because he's the only one involved in doing it, but to have five guys doing this at the same time is much more complex. Coleman avoided using a piano after his first recording session but we were making a group music where harmony was spontaneously produced with the piano as an integral part. We made a harmonic entity out of it, something pleasant to the ear. Getting rid of the piano was like saying, 'You can't be free *and* have harmony. It's one or the other.' But that isn't so.

When I first heard Ornette's music, honestly I didn't think much of it. At that time, anyway, I couldn't grasp what he was doing. Some of it I couldn't understand at all. It didn't stir feelings in me because I think that music must have a melodic progression. In what he was doing there was no melody as such, no harmony, no fixed pattern. When you get three or four or five people playing together there has to be some *form* of harmony. If you've got that content, then I find, anyway, that it's much easier to understand. Just playing loads of notes, in itself, doesn't mean anything. The combination of sounds must mean something. It's difficult to explain. With our quintet we combined to try to produce an overall sound that would spark different musical feelings. That's why we could use free improvisation, modal improvisation and chord-based improvisation and mix them as we thought appropriate. We wanted to use the whole palette, the whole range of possibilities and be free to do that. That's what free form really means.

The bass player's role in Coleman's music was different from mine with Harriott. In Ornette's quartet the bassist – Charlie Haden, say – would usually be playing against a soloist, listening to one solo voice and playing according to that, but in our group there were several voices. I had to listen to the interplay between them and go in the direction they indicated, while keeping in fairly good harmony with the piano, because Pat and I were reacting to the horns as well as following each other. We listened closely so that if one made a move, the other would move to cover. It was always a relationship of the whole group, something the five of us tried to construct at every moment together, not a relationship between a solo voice and an accompanist.

When, several years later in 1965, Ornette first came to London to play at the Fairfield Hall in Croydon, Shake and I went to see him at his hotel in Queensway. We chatted with him while he finished some material for the concert. He was writing music while he talked. I didn't understand how anybody could do that. I'm sure he knew about our involvement with free music although I can't recall a single word he said at that meeting. But I do remember being aghast at the way he was working. How can you be talking about general things and, at the same time, writing music intended to connect to people? It gave me the idea that it didn't matter much what he wrote so long as it sounded odd: that his aim in life was just to sound odd – not particularly to make any sense but to sound odd, which to me his music does most of the time.

Anyway, at the beginning of the 1960s we had something important in common with Ornette. Over the next few years, our music in Britain, like his in America, would become a focus of bitter controversy that divided the jazz scene. Like him we were going to suffer a lot of abuse for what we were trying to do and life was about to become very tough indeed.

9.

swallows on the water

When the *Abstract* album was released in 1963 the leading American jazz magazine *Down Beat* reviewed it and gave a top rating of five stars. That was a huge boost for us. It represented real recognition of what we were trying to do. The most prestigious journal in jazz was saying our record was one of the most important around. That vote of confidence came at a time when we badly needed it.

As well as the usual regular gigs, we sometimes played at Ronnie Scott's Old Place in Gerrard Street and it was a funny situation. When we played free form there, the musicians listening or drinking at the bar would creep out and stand at the doorway, looking aghast. You could see those puzzled – 'What on earth are they doing?' – expressions on their faces. Ronnie and Pete King were usually looking after business but a lot of other musicians reacted in a completely negative way. They couldn't understand at all and many were openly scoffing.

When I listen now to the records we made, I find it hard to understand why there was quite so much controversy. Time changes things. It's a matter of getting your ears used to different combinations of sounds. In all music throughout the ages certain sounds have been fashionable and if you didn't follow that fashion people wouldn't understand. When we recorded *Free Form* and *Abstract* I knew we were trying to make a *big* revolution in jazz because of people's reaction to that music. Many found it extraordinary and confusing. A lot told us straight out what they thought and called our music rubbish. And people would ask me quietly 'What are you doing? Why are you involved in all this?' Even today there are people who say they can't understand it. It all depends on their musical experience which might not be wide enough. Perhaps they've always followed narrow lines of appreciation in music.

But I believe that the best of that free form stuff we did is timeless music. It's unique and not tied to the era in which it was made. Bach's work – his 'Preludes', for example – is absolutely timeless, beautiful, a unique style. Nobody else made music like that, composing like Bach did. That's what I mean by timeless. And, in jazz, Joe was ahead of his time.

He tried to be upbeat about reactions to free form and he was always very determined. The notes he wrote for *Abstract* have an almost defiant tone: 'On dates all over the country we have found that we get better receptions for this kind of music than we do for conventional modern jazz, strangely enough. I am not saying free form will replace the music which makes up the general scene. But it will build up quite a following. It's here to stay.' And we did find that audiences were happy with a certain amount of it, mixed into the programme alongside the more conventional jazz from the old repertoire. Some listeners accepted free form without any preconceptions, which was always what we had hoped would happen. At the Marquee there was a mixed reception but enough people were very enthusiastic about it to encourage us. At concerts or club appearances we always included free form in the programme and Joe gradually increased the proportion because people began asking us to play particular free form compositions. That was very gratifying up to a point.

It was criticism from established musicians that was so demoralising. We thought they should have been able to understand what we were *trying* to do and treat it sympathetically even if they thought we weren't approaching it in the right way. But often their reaction was one of astonishment and sometimes complete mockery. Their experience of music was a strict regime of barlines and chord sequences and if you strayed from that they didn't think you were playing music at all. The *Down Beat* review helped us to believe in ourselves, to believe we weren't playing rubbish. Harvey Pekar, the reviewer, emphasised 'notable differences' between our music and what Ornette was doing, the significance of the way the piano was used in Harriott's group conception and the importance of Pat's contribution. The review was very important to us in letting us know that the local criticism we were getting wasn't everything. There were people elsewhere, knowledgeable about a wide range of jazz, who thought our music was worth listening to.

Apart from local musicians' reactions, what was disappointing was that the music didn't impress people who were in a position to promote it. They mattered because as a musician you play for the public and want them to hear what you are doing. If it is not promoted by people who have the responsibility for presenting music, the general public may not know anything about it. At the Marquee we could play whatever we liked but among the recording companies and in the broadcasting media we were never in any demand at all. It was only through Denis Preston that Joe's free form jazz was recorded. Without Denis all that music would have been lost.

***

In continental Europe there were much more positive reactions. Attitudes seemed more open there and that was one reason Joe always loved playing on the Continent. The quintet was booked to appear at a three day international jazz festival in Ascona in Switzerland in 1963. Our set was scheduled for Saturday August 17th, the middle day of the festival, and I drove to Switzerland in my car with Shake as a passenger.

Ascona is on the shore of Lake Maggiore and the town nestles by the foothills of the mountains in a very picturesque spot. But for those three days it rained continuously and the place was completely waterlogged. We played on the site of a small airfield and little planes would regularly come over the top of the hills and swoop down to land in this field. The rainwater poured in torrents down the hillsides and flooded the area around the stage. Eventually it reached the level of the stage and flowed on to it so that conditions were very uncomfortable. Later the rain subsided a bit but it certainly interrupted the proceedings.

It didn't dampen people's spirits too much, however. The international lineup for the festival included saxophonists Bud Shank and Dick Morrissey, blues singer Champion Jack Dupree, Chris Barber's band with Ottilie Patterson, the Albert Mangelsdorff Quintet, the Don Rendell Quintet, South African pianist Abdullah Ibrahim (then known as Dollar Brand), and British organist Graham Bond. Musicians from France, Austria, Italy and Switzerland appeared too. We played our usual mix of hard bop, ballads and free form and Albert Mangelsdorff talked with us after we had played and said he had much enjoyed our set. He and his group were enthusiastic and interested in the way our music was developing (he had heard us four years before at San Remo) and they were very attentive listeners when we played.

Albert is now recognised as one of the greatest trombon-
ists in jazz. At that time he had a very competent group
using arrangements in standard style although done in the
band's own way. But probably something he heard from us
at Ascona added a bit of encouragement to him to think
about reorganising his group's music along more adventurous lines, adding in freer elements. During the year following Ascona, he started playing his own new, expressive style
of powerful, driving free jazz and the Albert Mangelsdorff
Quintet with Heinz Sauer on tenor, altoist Günter
Kronberg, bassist Günter Lenz and drummer Ralf Hübner
became a great European group, often said to be one of the
best of its era. I think we could have been an influence on
that change of style. What we were doing was certainly
noticed by European musicians in those years and later, and
it helped to inspire new approaches that contributed to the
distinctiveness of European free jazz styles in the 1960s and
1970s. In fact Joe is sometimes called the father of
European free jazz. Young musicians on the Continent
were receptive to what we were trying to do.

Europe was important in that way. It provided a different
focus. We felt that it wasn't always necessary to look to
America for the next idea in jazz. That was a revolutionary
idea then but became a widespread view among the most
adventurous young European jazz musicians over the following years. Joe said in an interview in the year we went to
Ascona that he had 'a pet hate,' the idea 'that one couldn't
think for oneself unless one emigrated to a place like the
United States.' He thought this had 'not necessarily helped
people to be more inventive. They look to a place for a
guide.' But if 'one is able to stand back and look at the situation, one could be easily encouraged to think for oneself.
There shouldn't be one place leading the thinking public or
the musicians or aspiring artists.' In his buttoned-up, for-

mal, measured way he was talking about something we all
felt deeply.

During 1963 we went back to Lansdowne to record again.
But it was impossible to ignore the fact that free form was
not a commercial proposition. For all the acclaim *Abstract*
received in the United States and the encouragement from
some quarters, the records presumably were not selling in
large enough numbers. Someone decided that our next LP,
entitled *Movement*, should be a mix of free form and conventional pieces. I don't think Denis Preston was behind
that decision: he always supported whatever we wanted to
do. Probably Joe reluctantly concluded that it was a necessary strategy. And, of course, it reflected the usual mix in
our live performances.

Three of Joe's free form compositions were included on
the *Movement* album and they show further ways in which
the group could interact. 'Spaces' presents unaccompanied
statements by each instrument in turn and emphasises the
use of silences. The title track 'Movement' conjures up a
circular movement of the music around the group, like a
ball being thrown from each person to the next. 'Beams'
with its sequence of four, then six, seven and eight repeat-
ed notes in the theme (perhaps like flashing beams from a
lighthouse) has fast, complex interaction over a slow-medi-
um loping rhythm. In complete contrast to those pieces, a
version of 'Count Twelve', the calypso tune 'Revival' and
the relaxed 'Morning Blue' were also included – all written
by Joe and very much standard repertoire. The remaining
items were two compositions by our friend Michael
Garrick.

Michael was mainly known as a pianist then. We got to
know him particularly because he led a small band at the
Marquee when we played there. It was a quartet that
included vibraphonist Peter Shade. His band and ours were

on the bill together each week for several months. So there was the chance to hear each other's music regularly. Michael was very sympathetic to Joe's free form ideas and later often played Joe's compositions with his own groups. He wrote a free form piece called 'A Face in the Crowd' which we played on *Movement*. His other tune on the album was 'Blues on Blues', an attractive, simple blues theme relying heavily on Shake's use of a mute.

Because I saw little of Joe offstage and didn't talk much with him I didn't know exactly how the general reactions to free form affected him. At one level, as long as we were happy playing it he was fine. But it was obvious that he was disappointed, as all of us were, that what we thought of as exciting musical ideas full of possibilities were not getting much recognition. Frank Holder, who knew Joe as well as anyone on a personal level, once said in an interview that he thought the sense of rejection preyed on Joe's mind a lot. 'I was living in Earls Court... and he used to come to my house. He'd ring me up at one or two o'clock in the morning – "Frank, can I come over, man?" I'd say, yes, come. We'd have a bottle of Scotch and he used to drink and talk. He was very, very depressed and, in fact, on the phone I realised that if I hadn't seen him any of these times he might have done something.' Joe was such a loner that he had few resources to fall back on, except his own powerful sense of self-reliance, his impenetrable hard shell.

It gradually became obvious that we could not take free form any further in those years. *Movement* was the last record by the quintet which contained any of Joe's 'abstract music'. His disillusionment was such that he gave up writing new material for the group. In club and concert appearances we played jazz standards, ballads and the well-tried repertoire like 'Count Twelve'. But we needed something fresh to record.

Pat Smythe took it on himself to produce all the material

for the quintet's next album, made at Lansdowne in
September 1964. He didn't actually compose the eight
pieces on the record. They originated as songs from a musi-
cal called 'High Spirits', which had been very successful on
Broadway in New York and then in London at the Savoy
Theatre during 1964. It was based on Noel Coward's play
'Blithe Spirit' which had, itself, been a huge success in
London in the war years. Pat wrote jazz scores of Hugh
Martin's tunes, turning them into fine vehicles for the quintet. I still have a copy of the arrangements. Pat painstaking-
ly wrote them out in black ink in his incredibly neat script
and there's hardly an alteration on them, just two or three
scribbled-in changes that must have been made at the
recording session. After the *High Spirits* album was released
in 1965, *Jazz Journal's* reviewer wrote: 'Despite Harriott's
disclaimer (in the liner notes) that this is only "a slightly
jazzed-up version", there are no concessions to commercial-
ism. There is plenty of excellent improvising.... Though this
album may hold little interest for Harriott's free form
admirers, it could well appeal strongly to post-bop enthusi-
asts.' No doubt that was the idea. But *High Spirits* was the
last album the quintet made for Denis Preston.

As possibilities for the quintet narrowed, other playing and
recording situations arose to fill the space. From 1963 on, I
became increasingly involved with Michael Garrick's projects. Michael is a very adventurous musician, interested in
a wide variety of things. As a pianist he has an upfront,
attacking style, practically never laid back. But he also has
a lot of vision and sometimes produces really beautiful
things, especially the compositions he has written for choir
and organ. To be a composer you need imagination, you
can't compose by rote, and Michael has good ideas and has
written some good melodies. Also he had studied English at
university and was interested in poetry. He became very

involved in concerts combining poetry and jazz, writing melodies to support the words.

Since he liked the music of the Harriott quintet and our playing as individuals, he started to use Joe, Shake and me on his records and formed a quintet of his own that included the three of us. I owe a lot to him for involving me in the great breadth of the music he eventually encompassed and for having faith in me, as it were, at a time when that was needed. He brought different sounds into the music and a different approach. For example, jazz musicians are seldom interested in choral music and a lot of jazz people don't want to know about singing at all. But Michael eventually began to write compositions for choirs. He knew how to use them in a jazz setting and how to use a pipe organ in jazz-oriented works. It brought me right back home in a way because it reminded me of my father's work as an organist with choirs and, of course, you rarely hear a pipe organ in jazz, let alone have the chance to play alongside one.

One of the earliest of Michael's albums that I contributed to was *October Woman*, recorded at Decca's West Hampstead Studios for the Argo label in November 1964. That was lovely music. Shake and Joe were the front line and Colin Barnes was on drums. All the compositions were Michael's and since everyone was familiar with each other's playing it was an easy session, mainly just a matter of getting the recording balance right. I had been playing most of the pieces on gigs with Michael and they created no particular challenges, except perhaps 'Anthem' which was different from everything else on the record in incorporating some free form playing. Michael wanted to provide an opportunity for that in his composing. The piece was in 5/4 time.

Working with different time signatures in jazz was new to us then and improvising in 5/4, not a steady sequence of fours, feels strange at first. Similarly with 7/4: that's four and three. You feel, when you get to the three, that you should be going to four but you're not. You're going back to one. If you have been playing that rhythm for years it becomes natural, as in, say, Hungarian music, but the jazz musician feels natural in 4/4 time. The three throws you slightly off balance. In the early 1960s it was still unusual to play jazz in time signatures other than 4/4 or 3/4 but Michael's music often required that.

One reviewer, hearing 'Anthem', asked whether Joe and Shake were really committed to free form since they could apparently 'switch from conventional blowing to freedom stuff at will'. Were 'they being merely fashionable?' It was the strangest thing to say because how we played was always relative to what the composition required. It wasn't necessary to play everything the same way. But that was an example of the kind of misunderstanding that could be depressing if you paid heed to it. We had battled through a lot of hostility to try to develop free form. It wasn't anything to do with fashion.

Michael developed 'Anthem' further and recorded the composition again in April 1965 with the same quintet plus the Elizabethan Singers and organist Simon Preston. So, on that record, for the first time I played bass accompanying a pipe organ. Many of the organ's notes are in the double bass range but the sounds of the two instruments are distinct. If you are playing in a church there's plenty of space to create a separation and, in recording, the bass has a different tone from the organ: the organ is a wind tone and the bass has a different kind of vibration. Bowed bass gives a sound closer to that of the organ but bass notes can have more attack than organ notes. It's a subtle difference. Organ tones can fill the whole space but huge sounds can be produced from an amplified bass too. The combination can give tremendous depth to the sound of the music.

In later years, when Michael played pipe organ himself in performances of his large-scale compositions, he could get a different feel in his playing from what a classical organist would produce. I had no problems playing with him when he used the organ, because I felt I understood its sound and dynamics. In large part, of course, that was because of hearing my father playing the instrument so often when I was growing up. In fact, when I play bass I'm always thinking of producing a kind of organ sound like I heard in my youth. That lovely, rich sound is always in my head.

Apart from straight jazz appearances and recordings with Michael there were poetry and jazz presentations, in which he was very active. Having poems read to jazz accompaniment was an idea that caught on in the 1960s and early 1970s. It was the kind of thing arts centres liked and it built up a big following. Michael wasn't the first jazz musician to write music to accompany poetry reading in Britain. Tony Kinsey and Bill LeSage composed music for a broadcast and a record with the poet Christopher Logue in 1959. But the idea flourished from the early 1960s. Shake and Joe were a part of this side of Michael's activities before I was but after a while I joined Michael's trio which became the basic musical unit for the poetry and jazz events.

Michael was good at writing tunes to accompany the poetry, creating the right atmosphere. The main problem was that most readers – the poets themselves during those first years – were not used to the strict rhythms of jazz. They had to adjust to the musicians because the tempo of the music must be kept. But that's hard for someone who doesn't have a feel for jazz rhythm. It was often difficult for the reader to enter at the right moment and pace the reading with the music. And they had to be able to speak the lines in a way that flowed. That's a difficult art but when it worked it was effective.

The poet Jeremy Robson was a prime mover in all that activity in those years and we played many concerts and recorded with him. But I didn't think he had the particular feel needed for the jazz although he obviously put much thought into the relationship between the words and the music. He wrote, in notes for one of the records, that his poems were 'deliberately simple and flexible in form, intended to reflect and respond to the rhythms of jazz – for it is essential to give the musicians scope to play creatively, so that the jazz is not merely an accompaniment but rather one of two elements forming an entirely new compound. But of course, as Michael Garrick says, "words are more or less precise in their meaning, whereas musical phrases are not, so that when the two come together it is necessarily the poetry which defines the emotional area to be explored."' That's must be right. The music must conform to the meaning of the poem.

Michael's trio toured the country with poetry and jazz and I was involved with this activity through to the 1970s. Colin Barnes was usually the drummer and while he didn't have a flashy technique he did what was needed and was fine for poetry and jazz. Eventually, rather than relying on the poets themselves to read their work we brought in a single reader to work regularly with the trio. That was Betty Mulcahy who joined us in March 1971 and appeared with the trio at poetry and jazz events for several years after that. She was a marvellous reader and great interpreter of poetry, although not a poet herself. Even Betty couldn't feel the time of a blues, however, and on one piece we did she would almost reach the end of the poem before the blues was ending. She had to draw out the words to try to keep the poem going to the end of the music, so it didn't quite gel. Those kinds of things were always a problem because jazz and poetry are rhythmically very different.

Among the poets, John Smith was unlike the others

because he listened carefully to the way we sounded and wrote for us as musicians in 'Jazz for Five', a set of poems with each member of Michael's quintet in mind. Michael put music to John's words and each instrument alone accompanied the reader. One poem, 'Blue Dusk', was for me and that was very exciting. I remember a phrase – 'He ran out crying' – which was part of Joe's poem and his alto accompanied it with a sort of anguished wailing: expressing how he felt along with the words. On pieces like that the combination of music and poetry could be powerful and the poems were sometimes very inspiring. Poetry is not vital to me – I can take it or leave it – but when I hear good poetry, well read, it can certainly affect me. I'd rather hear it read aloud than read it myself, as long as there is an experienced reader who knows how to extract the nuances. I always enjoyed listening to Shake reading his poetry because he had a great sense of rhythm and timing.

There was yet another side of Michael's work which I first became involved with in the mid-1960s and stayed with for many years. His trio started to take music to schools. Michael knew Victor Fox who was a jazz fan and eventually became Assistant Music Director for Hampshire schools. Victor had a budget to promote music in education and suggested to Michael that we might bring his trio to play in the schools. We started with a concert at a primary school in Hampshire, playing to the children, aged five or six upwards, and encouraging them to make music for us, singing and playing their percussion instruments. If they knew and liked a particular song we would play it with them, encouraging them to listen for various features in the music, and Michael was very good at explaining everything to the children.

He reminded me recently of one special event we did and of how well Victor Fox related to the children. Some time in the late 1960s, Victor arranged for the children from several schools to join together to sing at a concert in a music festival at Hamble near Southampton. There were maybe four or five schools with several hundred children all combined into one huge choir. At the rehearsal they were singing the national anthem. Michael played the piano introduction and the children started but after a few bars Victor Fox stopped them. 'This is the Queen's song, isn't it?' he said. 'Where does the Queen live?' 'In London,' they chorused. 'Will she be able to hear that?' 'No!' 'Then sing louder!' And they all sang at the tops of their voices for the Queen. Everthing had to be done lightly, with a lot of humour, but, as Michael put it, 'real humour, not talking down to the children at all.'

We made many school visits, usually arriving around lunchtime or early afternoon so that the music was a break for the children before they got tired. Those events made me think that it is important that children should have the chance to hear a wide range of music and sing or play an instrument at an early age. It's part of their birthright and music should be part of their lives. They can learn to express themselves through it and playing or singing together also teaches them to cooperate with other people, contributing something to a big whole.

Victor Fox's budget was quite generous so we were well paid and worked around Hampshire for a decade or more. In the mid-1970s the funding situation changed so it came to an end. But it was a good experience while it lasted.

During the first half of the 1960s the Joe Harriott Quintet continued in existence. But it gradually became harder to find outlets for the music that had made the group unique. And musically, we had become extremely dependent on each other. Joe's kind of free form was only possible with musicians in perfect empathy – like swallows on the water, as he might have put it. If any of the group were missing it couldn't work properly. That had been shown clearly when Shake left temporarily at the end of 1960 to finish his English literature studies at London University. While he was away from the the group through most of 1961, Les Condon took his place. Les is a fine trumpeter but he didn't have a feeling for free form and wasn't convinced about it although he did his best until Shake returned.

There is recorded evidence of how things turned out in that period because tapes from a concert the quintet played in Manchester in January 1961 have been issued on the *Joe Harriott: Genius* CD. Two free form compositions, 'Coda' and 'Tempo' are included. If Shake had been playing, there would have been much improvised interplay between the horns but that doesn't happen on those recordings. When Les Condon improvises, Joe comes in, trying to be a foil for him as he would with Shake. But Les was used to situations where each person takes a turn in the solo spotlight. So when Joe improvises, Les stays quiet. The music becomes a series of solos without the tension that came when Shake and Joe interacted. But Joe's words at the end of the concert show that he was gratified by the warm applause the free form performances received from the large audience.

Without Shake the quintet's music could not reach the quality we aspired to. So when he finally left the group in 1965 to move to Germany it was a huge blow. His leaving wasn't a complete surprise and I had feared it would happen. There wasn't the work there had been, bookings for the quintet gradually diminished, Joe was drinking more by that time and personal relations between Joe, Shake and me were becoming strained. There were so many disappointments to face.

Shake's marriage had broken up and, despite all his musical talent, he was not making an adequate living in London. For one thing, being a brandy drinker is expensive and his habit was heavy. He had had the chance to make records under his own name, including a Columbia EP *In My Condition* that used the personnel of the Harriott quintet. But he was frustrated that he had not received the recognition he wanted and clearly deserved. So he took a job with Kurt Edelhagen's radio orchestra in Cologne. He became the star of that band and worked with other groups on the Continent, including the wonderful Kenny Clarke-Francy Boland Big Band.

In 1973 he went back to St. Vincent because a friend of his in the government invited him to become Director of Culture. But then the government changed again and in 1975 the Department of Culture he had set up was abolished and he lost his position. He had an unhappy stint running a college and then moved to New York in 1980, no doubt hoping to get into the centre of jazz activity there. But for a long time he didn't have a work permit and struggled with whatever musical jobs he could find, playing with West Indian bands and writing music for them. He wasn't happy living in Brooklyn but he stayed, making occasional visits abroad until he died in 1997. The lady who was his companion in New York in the last years was also from St Vincent and I think he knew her from home.

For me, Shake's leaving for Germany in 1965 was a great personal blow. He had lived in my house for about four years. We would listen to music and drink together. When we were both touring with the quintet we often travelled together. After he left we were always in contact and he would phone me every month or so from the States, right up to the end. He died on a visit to Norway and I went, with Gertrude and all the family Shake had in London, to his funeral in Oslo.

I remember the way he used to talk about women, relationships, music, his childhood and youth, and about West Indian things. He used to tell me about the volcano he climbed, behind the place where he had grown up in St. Vincent. He wrote a poem about it. Of course, I remembered the mountains in Jamaica too. I could share his West Indian approach to life. It's hard to explain what that is but it's to do with having lived where the sea and the sun are always nearby. That engenders a different emotion in people, something that those who never see the sea cannot possibly feel or understand. It's to do with climate: the air and the light. The light is brighter in the Caribbean. Your body feels different. Houses are open, not enclosed, the wind blows through, people drop in, calling on each other unannounced. You are freer, in touch with the elements, close to everything in nature.

We felt the same way about how to bring up children and about relationships between children and parents. He had had a strict upbringing like mine. We both had been made to feel that you had to earn your place in society. He came to Britain to study English as I came to study engineering. The original idea for people like us coming from the Caribbean then was always to go back: not to see if you could make your way better here, but to learn something and take that knowledge back home. But then, of course, other influences come in and things change in your outlook. I settled down and found a way of life. Perhaps in that respect Shake was more of a wanderer.

I worked with him again in 1989 when he came to Britain to play in a quintet Michael Garrick put together for some concerts to celebrate Joe Harriott's music. Bobby Orr and altoist Martin Hathaway were in the group, too. But Shake was just a pale shadow of his old musical self. His embouchure was in poor shape, his technique was hesitant and there were only rare hints of anything like the old brilliance. But he kept on writing beautiful poetry right up to the end. Just a few months before he died, he sent from New York a poem in four verses. It was dated 'Brooklyn, Jan

1997' and he had written in long-hand at the end of the typescript, 'For Gertrude and Cole, a thank-offering. Shake'. The poem, called 'Angel Horn', reads as an elegy for his musical life and much more. It begins:

> When I was born
> my father gave to me
> an angel-horn
> with wings of melody.
> That angel placed her lips
> upon my finger-tips,
> and I became, became
> her secret name.

And ends:

> Now light is low,
> new angels come and go.
> The passion-tree
> spreads dense as destiny.
> But this old angel-horn
> strives like the lifting dawn.
> Love moves to claim, to claim
> our secret name.

Shake's leaving for Germany really meant the end of the Harriott Quintet. Nobody could replace him. The feel of the group was completely destroyed. After that, Joe used other excellent trumpeters, such as Ian Carr and Kenny Wheeler, but the band could never be the same and it didn't work often. Unexpectedly, however, one more quintet recording did take place, in June 1967, with Stu Hamer on trumpet and Phil Seamen back again on drums for that one session. It happened because the jazz record shop owner Doug Dobell liked Harriott's hard bop music and set up the date. But it was as though things had come full circle. The music on the record was the kind of repertoire we had used in 1958 and included some of the same tunes. It was almost a throwback to the idiom of

Harriott's first quintet but having Pat on piano made a big difference as far as I was concerned.

I enjoyed the session. It was in a pokey little independent studio somewhere in east London. Neither the piano nor the recording equipment were very good and at the beginning the engineer couldn't get a decent bass sound. But eventually the sound quality wasn't bad and somehow that session had a spark. Joe plays so fiercely on the record that at times it seems as though he is about to blow his alto apart. But he also contributes a lovely, gentle performance of 'Polka Dots and Moonbeams'. Stu Hamer was keen to make the most of the session and played at his best. He and his brother Ian, also a trumpeter, were sons of a lady who owned a Liverpool ballroom where the quintet had sometimes appeared, so that was how Joe knew about him.

Phil's health worried me a lot that day. He was in a bad way and I thought he didn't have long to live (in fact he died in 1972). But, as always, he sounded good: he was incapable of playing badly and I'm glad he made that date because it was the last ever recording session of Joe's quintet. It was good to be in the studio together again as a band but it felt strange without Shake. Anyway, I knew the recording was a one-off and that the quintet would not get back together again. Anything else would have been like starting afresh. Once something has run its course you can't recreate it.

10.

rich tapestry

As the independent existence of the Joe Harriott Quintet was coming to an end, other unusual musical possibilities opened up. In Britain, as elsewhere, the 1960s and early 1970s were years when a lot of artistic experimenting went on. People explored new ideas and made connections that had not been tried before between different idioms in music and between music and the other arts.

Poetry and jazz was one of those new movements, but I was involved with other determined attempts to stretch artistic boundaries in music during that time. One of them was the composer David Mack's unique *New Directions* album on the Columbia label, recorded with a nine piece group in 1964 and released the following year. On it, Mack used twelve-tone rows instead of familiar chord sequences as a basis for jazz, applying the serial technique that had been employed in classical composition by Arnold Schoenberg and others to replace orthodox harmony. Basically this involves using a particular fixed sequence of the notes of the chromatic scale to provide the foundation for all aspects of a composition. Whether it was an important record is hard to judge because the actual playing was not all that wonderful. Mack used some older musicians with a rather stilted style of playing which perhaps didn't do justice to the music. But it was a real innovation. No-one had used twelve-tone composition in such a thoroughgoing, ambitious way in a jazz setting before.

I don't know how the record came about or why I was contacted to play on it but probably it was because of my experience with free form. Mack would have heard Harriott's records and perhaps he was inspired to use the serial technique as another way to escape the limitations of chord sequences as a basis for jazz. Shake Keane was still in Britain at the time the record was made and he was the main soloist on the album.

It was very difficult music to play and every note had to be read throughout each piece: as far as my bass part was concerned there was no chance to improvise. I know nothing about the theory of serial music and don't particularly like some serial compositions that I've heard. But for a person involved with jazz to want to use this technique was unexpected and intriguing. Mack found how to do it and with Shake he had an improviser who could rise to the challenge, using his tremendous ear and abundant imagination. But the music gave me no freedom. I had the notes to play, the serial progression, and I had to connect them to the rest of the harmonic content of the music at each moment in performance but the notes seemed strange, not a progression that obviously made sense harmonically. So, not being able to feel a natural harmony I had to concentrate very much on my intonation. As a result I felt inhibited in producing the music. It needed one hundred percent concentration.

Mack's experiment was a well kept secret and his record made little impact. Perhaps serial technique was just too difficult as a basis for jazz improvising. But a few years later a different kind of musical breakthrough captured the popular imagination and gained a lot of publicity for a while. Nowadays fusions of jazz with 'world music' and folk or traditional music styles of all kinds are commonplace but in the late 1960s the concept of linking jazz and Indian music, with which I became much involved at that time, was revolutionary. Pat Smythe had played music with some Indian musicians and I think it was mostly his influence that brought about the Indo-Jazz Fusions project. But the prime mover in developing the idea was an Indian violinist and composer named John Mayer who had studied Western music and was keen to find ways of combining its techniques with those of Indian classical music.

In 1965 at the Lansdowne Studios, Denis Preston introduced Mayer to Joe Harriott who must have been looking for new ideas to record. The idea took shape for a 'double quintet' that would combine a jazz group led by Harriott with a small group of Indian musicians. Mayer devised the overall musical conception using jazz phrasing and improvisation in a framework of Indian raga form and he wrote pieces for the group to play.

Joe was happy to go along with all that. It was a new challenge and he liked challenges. His own revolutionary project – free form – had run down and could no longer be pursued as a practical matter. So he became co-leader of the double quintet with Mayer, and Pat Smythe and I joined it. In fact one of Joe's old free form pieces, 'Subject', was adapted for the group and recorded on the second Indo-Jazz Fusions album in September 1966, but otherwise the music was new and driven by John Mayer's ideas.

John Mayer is a good musician, classically trained. He grew up in Calcutta and came to London to pursue his violin studies at the Royal Academy of Music. He plays the instrument very well and has worked in symphony orchestras. Being thoroughly familiar with the Indian raga form, he knew how to write the parts for the music and produced them all. John has a quick mind and very quick way of talking and is quite a jolly person. That was useful as some of the Indian musicians were tricky personalities and he knew how to smooth out problems. Because he understood the Indian instruments he could suggest how a certain passage might be played, for example on the sitar, and get the musicians in the right frame of mind. Some of them were doubtful about fusing the musical idioms but with his pleasant personality he could reassure them.

Many difficult practical problems arose in bringing together jazz and Indian music. The Indian instruments – the sitar and the tabla drums, for example – are quiet by comparison with the trumpet, alto saxophone and jazz drums. That caused considerable problems in recording. The jazz drums had to be suppressed while the Indian instruments played, so as not to drown them out. Then later, in the middle of the piece, the drums could play more forcefully when the jazz musicians improvised. So the volume of each instrument had to be controlled. The jazz instruments generally had to fade down, except for me, because everyone needed to hear clearly the raga notes which the bass played to provide the structure of the piece.

For live performances we would mike up as much as possible, amplifying the different instruments. Otherwise, in a big hall or theatre, some of the players wouldn't be heard at all. With all those complications it was hard to know how the instrumental balance sounded in the auditorium, so at rehearsal before a concert somebody would always go to the back of the hall and check the sound. Apart from everything else, it was sometimes hard for the jazz musicians to hear the Indian players properly. They would sit on the floor cross-legged on a carpet which absorbed some of the sound. The group's flautist Chris Taylor became a kind of bridge between the Indian players and the jazz. When the double quintet started he was not sure how to tackle this music but eventually he played wonderfully.

In fact, Indian music is very formal indeed when based on the raga, which is really a series of scales. My task was to lay down the lines of the raga and keep it going right through the performance, except when a point for free jazz improvisation had been reached. That needed discipline. It's not like playing chords in jazz but more like a part in a classical composition though with less musical variation. In classical music the bass part accompanies the changing melodic line presented by the soloist or the other instruments in the orchestra. But the raga is a series of notes which I had to play in a strict order. Sometimes the sitar played them along with me. The improvisers could dart about in the scale but had to use those notes. Effectively it's modal improvising. A melody could be played in Indian style with the Indian rhythm section and then, as the sitar dropped out of the music, the jazz musicians could begin to improvise with the jazz rhythm section and the Indian rhythm instruments. Mayer wrote all the bass lines and having to play an entirely pre-determined line throughout a piece was very different from normal jazz practice – though not so different, I suppose, from what was required on David Mack's album.

The music required much rehearsing. But the Indian musicians didn't need to be present while we tried out jazz parts that did not involve them as soloists. In performance, they provided background rhythm for those parts. The sitar player, Diwan Motihar, played the melody but, assuming he had learned his part correctly, when the whole group got together the music would gel. So he would not usually need to come to our rehearsals. A few days before a concert or perhaps at the venue before the show there would be a single rehearsal of the whole group. Everyone would know their part from the written arrangements so the final rehearsal was just to make sure we would play together at the right tempo with the right feel of the piece.

With this way of operating it remained a *double* quintet: two separate groups that joined up to perform the music. And it was not easy. I had to perfect my part because the notes I played from the raga defined the whole structure. Also, some time signatures that jazz musicians don't often use were involved. The raga might be based on patterns of nine, eleven or even thirteen beats. I didn't study Indian music as such but I did enjoy trying to understand what was involved in playing, thinking it out.

It was vital to have a rock-steady beat to hold the group tightly together, to keep a jazz swing and to have precise transitions from each section of the music to the next. The easiest of the Indian instruments to play with was the drone, the tamboura. But the tabla drums would sometimes get out of tempo, dragging or racing, and then it became hard to hold the steady pulse. Allan Ganley or Jackie Dougan who played jazz drums with the group had to face this problem too. I think Indian musicians often don't feel the need to emphasise the steady tempos that are so vital for jazz. They are concerned with an overall feel and if the tempo wobbles a bit it doesn't matter too much.

The Indo-Jazz Fusions were first presented to the public at a major concert at Chichester Festival Theatre in May 1966. It was an attractive little theatre, almost round, and the concert went well and attracted notice. I was not on the Harriott-Mayer group's first record but I played on the two subsequent albums. We also did several television broadcasts and festivals including the Isle of Wight and Bologna in Italy where we appeared with the singer Jon Hendricks. In Britain and abroad the music went down well, we did major concerts and the group attracted good coverage in the arts media. In a way it fitted the artistic fashions of the time. It presented an interesting, colourful spectacle on stage and had a musical style that was entirely new and sufficiently exotic to draw in a lot of people who might not have been attracted to jazz as such.

When Indo-jazz worked it could be exciting and some of the interplay was very intricate. It provided a welcome, fresh musical experience for me. Now and again you need to have something different to make you realise that there are many different approaches to playing music. It didn't provide anything like the degree of stimulation which Joe's quintet at its best had provided for me but it did create an altogether different musical sound and we were the first people to develop Indo-jazz in that way. It was another real musical breakthrough.

In 1971, not long after the Indo-Jazz Fusions band had finally broken up, Harriott summed it up casually in an interview: 'Some of the music was pretty. A pity it didn't work out. I liked a lot of it, you know, and learned a lot from it. It was fun breaking some of those rules.' By then, it seemed, he had tried everything in music and was a deeply disappointed man. Using someone else's musical conception, as in Indo-jazz, must have been no substitute for being able to pursue his own personal vision.

By the end of the 1960s he wasn't well physically and was finding it increasingly hard to control his drinking. One of his final performances with the Indo-Jazz Fusions was a concert in Northern Ireland. Getting there involved a flight from London and Joe was always terrified of flying. He got very drunk on the journey and when we went on stage for the concert in Belfast he could barely play. It wasn't a pretty sight and, after that, relations were very strained with John Mayer. In fact, when we did the final Indo-jazz recording with the double quintet Harriott wasn't on it. So I think he burnt his boats on that gig and that was how it all ended. The soul went out of the Indo-Jazz Fusions group – without Joe it no longer had a star – and the bookings for the band dried up.

***

Despite all Harriott's brilliance, his career went into a downward spiral after that. He spent his last few years travelling around the country playing with local rhythm sections, unable to afford to maintain a group of his own. He had never been able to develop a network of personal relationships in the music world that might have provided support when things became hard. In the end he was entirely on his own, just as he had always been. I lost touch with him and did not know what he was doing or how things were with him. But then, at the beginning of January 1973 when I was playing at a London night club called Gullivers, someone came in with the news that Joe had just died in Southampton, where he had been playing. He had had cancer and had spent his last days in the Wessex Radiotherapy Unit.

I think all the problems he had before, the pleurisy and the lung ailments, must have come back and he was too weakened to resist. His lungs would have been in a terrible state from the smoking and the recurrent infections and in the last few years he hadn't taken care of himself at all. He slept on people's floors, didn't eat properly and just travelled to wherever he could get a chance to play.

He was only 44 years old. His death came earlier than I had expected and it was a shock, but I wasn't entirely surprised because I knew how his health had been. His funeral was on January 10th and I went to Southampton for that. Michael Garrick played beautiful things on the organ and, in a way, it was a very lovely, moving occasion with maybe one or two hundred people. Ten days later, a benefit was held for Harriott at Gullivers to help cover the funeral expenses. Occasionally, later, I used to see Joe's daughter at some of Michael Garrick's concerts. She was a lovely young woman and he had a son, too, who lived in Germany. I met him just once, probably in that period soon after his father died.

Joe's death marked the end of an era and of many high hopes. Ian Carr wrote in his book *Music Outside* that 'Harriott... was defeated and worn down... by the system, by the hostile environment.' Ian had worked with Joe and known him. To the outside world, Harriott did not show his feelings but changes in his manner and his demeanour gave indications. In the last years I knew him, he was not at all the same chap who had started out. All of us involved in his projects felt his pain. We felt it was a terrible shame that the people who had the power to present, broadcast, explain and publicise his music often ignored or neglected it.

In the end, unfortunately, one puts it down to the fact that Joe wasn't a white Englishman. Had he been one, things would have been different. There can be no other explanation. A similar thing happened years before to Lauderic Caton and it's not easy to take but I suppose it's understandable because it is part of the culture and always has been. When it happens one can't be too surprised. In America, black musicians have received some recognition. They are a majority in jazz there, whereas in Britain they are a small minority and what they have done has been easier to ignore. But at least some of the music is on record.

Apart from Indo-Jazz Fusions and David Mack's serial jazz, the most innovatory musical experiences I was involved with in the late 1960s and 1970s were Michael Garrick's big choral projects. Michael wrote extremely ambitious works combining jazz groups with choirs and a highspot in this activity was the performance of his work 'Jazz Praises' at St. Paul's Cathedral in London in 1968. Trumpeter Ian Carr, saxophonists Art Themen and Jim Philip, drummer John Marshall and I were involved as the jazz group, with Michael playing the massive cathedral pipe organ. The choir was made up of children and teachers from a school we had visited with the trio, together with singers from two other choirs. The children loved performing because it was a new, special experience for them but there had to be a lot of rehearsal for such a large, complicated piece with so many elements involved. I seem to remember that the jazz group rehearsed at Art Themen's home in Kentish Town. The children had rehearsals at their school and then everybody involved in the performance met for full rehearsals at least a couple of times before we gave the public performance, because the piece needed a lot of co-ordination. Michael organised everything and it must have involved him in a great deal of work.

The St. Paul's concert was recorded with just a single dynamic microphone which I set up. I suspended it on a rope inside the dome of the cathedral above the choir and the instrumentalists so that it didn't pick up the echo from the roof and walls of the building but caught sound only from below. Michael spent all his available funds on a recording system and the resources would only extend to the one £8 microphone. But the quality of the recorded sound was good: the choir, the thundering organ, John Marshall's powerful drums, the bass and the horns all seemed to get a good balance. The band was placed between two sets of organ pipes and Michael, at the organ, was about twenty feet above the rest of the musicians so it was hard to play together because of the placing of the instruments.

Of course there was no recording engineer. Michael had to set up the recording himself and just let the tape run. It's amazing that the music was captured so well. The results came out on an LP issued by a small record company called Airborne, run by Noel Brown who had also been responsible for some of Shake's recordings. Some years later, Noel died and the Airborne label no longer exists, so that remarkable *Jazz Praises* album is very hard to find nowadays.

Later, Michael wrote an even more ambitious piece: a jazz cantata called 'Mr. Smith's Apocalypse'. The Mr. Smith was John Smith, the poet with whom we had been involved in poetry and jazz events. He wrote the words for the cantata. John was very well off and well spoken, sounding definitely a class above everyone else, and dressed nattily. He made his living as a literary agent and had a lovely house in Brighton. 'Mr. Smith's Apocalypse' was recorded for Argo in 1971 and at about that time we took it on tour around the country. In a programme for the tour Michael explains how he began work on the composition:

> In April 1968, I received through the post the first twenty lines or so of a work [that] John Smith and I had decided would be about man's predicament in his relationship to God in the twentieth century.... I went that morning to the church of St. Michael the Archangel in Aldershot to practise the organ for our forthcoming St. Paul's Cathedral concert [of 'Jazz Praises'] and to begin work on the lines I had received from John Smith. On the same day, the news of the assassination of Martin Luther King shocked the world. Over the music I had been composing, I wrote this dedication, 'The Gateway of Sorrow: For Martin Luther King'.

'Mr. Smith's Apocalypse' was beautiful music. The group performing it on the Argo recording included trumpeter Henry Lowther, singer Norma Winstone, Don Rendell and Art Themen on reeds, drummer Trevor Tomkins and a large choir, again including schoolchildren with other singers. We also performed it at a concert in Westminster Hall in London and recorded it for a BBC radio broadcast. It was a great musical success and after that Michael wrote several more lovely choral pieces. His work deserves to be better known because it is often highly imaginative. He deserves much more recognition. But there were no big star names attached to those choral works, nothing sensational to attract commercial interest and all the money that is needed to mount and promote things of that scale.

***

We pushed musical boundaries with Michael's projects, Indo-Jazz Fusions and things like David Mack's serial jazz. All of that was enjoyable but I needed everyday bread and butter work to rely on, playing situations that were perhaps less glamorous but brought in a steady income and were satisfying enough musically. So all through this time I had other playing commitments.

I was with Alan Clare at the Studio Club quite often and, for maybe a couple of years around 1965, I worked with a quartet at the Georgian Club off Piccadilly. Then around 1970 I played regularly with pianist Lennie Felix at the Pickwick Club. That was a nightclub in Little Newport Street which attracted artists and film and show business people. The regulars included the actor John Hurt and Johnny Speight, the TV scriptwriter, who liked to sit in on drums sometimes. We played jazz sets before and after the cabaret and the Deniz brothers who worked nearby at the Talk of the Town would sometimes come by to sit in with us. Lennie was exciting to play with but eccentric and notoriously short-tempered. When the American cornettist Ruby Braff worked with him Braff said in despair, 'I asked for a piano player and they gave me a disease'. Lennie had strong views about drummers and a lot didn't get invited back after working with him once. And woe betide any guests doing the cabaret who couldn't read the musical parts. But he was a fine jazz player, always popular with audiences, and we got on well.

I also got occasional work over a long period in the 1960s and 1970s with Peter Ricardo, a flamboyant character from Grenada who sang calypsos and songs in West Indian style and played guitar. And, for many years, I did gigs for Jewish weddings and bar mitzvahs. George Fierstone had a band for those sorts of functions and I worked with him a lot. Most people playing that music are Jewish but maybe they included me because I'm sympathetic towards all sorts of music and knew most of what had to be played at those occasions.

In 1971 I started hotel work, which became my regular nightly job for around a dozen years, first at the Dorchester in Park Lane and later at the Churchill in Portman Square, both big international top-class hotels.

It began when I joined the trio that played in the Dorchester's restaurant when the main band took its break. Kenny Gordon, a drummer whom I had known since Caribbean Club days, played softly with brushes and sang well in a relaxed Nat 'King' Cole style. He had a lovely voice and I enjoyed working with him but the pianist-singer in the trio wasn't good technically and sounded corny although the diners seemed to like him. So we did a mix of sophisticated Nat Cole type numbers and very corny stuff.

The agent for the music was Geraldo. He supplied bands for the hotel and would sometimes sit in the restaurant while we played. And some regulars liked our music a lot. One lord who occasionally came for dinner hired the trio to play for a party he held at Ascot. Patrick Moore, the TV astronomer, sometimes came in too.

Is playing for diners in a hotel restaurant satisfying? It can certainly be a drag if they are noisy and take no interest. But if they like what you play you are doing the job well. The aim is to entertain people so you need to find what will appeal and excite them and that requires a big repertoire. One way is to get the waiter to ask guests if there is any-thing they would like the band to play. Communication is essential and the interesting part of the job was being able to entertain almost anyone with some music they enjoyed.

Making something for yourself out of what you're doing is important because if you don't enjoy it you can't transmit enjoyment to a listener. Starting with classical music as a boy gave me wide musical horizons. The many different possible musical categories and styles are all good in themselves and whether music in any of them is successful depends on how it is produced. The difference between good and bad is simply that good music touches your emotions. You can aim to make music like that in a jazz club, a concert hall or a hotel restaurant. That's what being professional is about.

There was little communication with the rest of the staff at the Dorchester. Each different department kept to itself. And the very self-important head doorman was someone I didn't get along with. Musicians never entered by the Dorchester Hotel's front door. I would go from the underground car park through the kitchens to the room where we changed into uniforms. That was convenient in a way but the idea was that everyone had to know their place. A sultan from the Far East lived in the hotel and always had his Rolls parked in a certain spot which everyone had to keep well away from. Plush hotels have their rituals, strict rules about this and that. They employ people to keep these rules for the high and mighty to make them feel important. After all, the guests are charged enough so they have to make them feel special. All part of the rich tapestry of life! But after a couple of years I was glad to move to the Churchill which was a happier place to work and where the musical environment was much better.

During the Dorchester period I did club work as well. Kenny Gordon also played at that time at a night club called L'Hirondelle and brought me in to the group, so after evening work at the hotel I would go on to play there. Later I worked at Gullivers night club for a few months and musicians would come by and sit in. Pat Smythe and Bill Le Sage were pianists there for various periods and those were lovely times. If something came up such as evening work with Michael Garrick or George Fierstone, I would sometimes put in a dep at the Dorchester which was easy to do because the music was very undemanding. The pianist-singer was the main draw and what he did was basically simple entertainment. Anyone who could play a few notes could dep there.

Things were completely different at the Churchill. The job was well paid and the group I was in was the resident quartet, called the Ten Four because we played in the Number Ten restaurant. I had to audition and the hotel's musical director and other top management sat around listening to check I was up to the job. That was in April 1973 and after that I played six nights a week there, with Sundays free, for ten years. The repertoire was very large and elaborate so it was hard to put in deps and we were definitely expected to be there to play every night. We would start at about 8.00 p.m. and break for a meal sometime between nine and ten. Then we were supposed to work until midnight but if there were important guests we would keep on playing until they left and they would always give tips or buy us drinks. But if the restaurant wasn't busy we would often be allowed to go home early.

The Ten Four's library of arrangements covered every style of music. It was a highly professional little group and we prided ourselves on the range of what we could do. One New Yorker who dined in the restaurant sent us a little note that read:

> The social rules seem to indicate that one does not applaud in this establishment. But I would like you four talented gentlemen to know that, if allowed, I would clap wildly. A great show! And a thank you. John Steffans.

Japanese diners were very surprised when we would notice them and begin to play Japanese music. But we used music of all kinds from all over the world to cater for the restaurant's international clientele. The hotel never told us to follow any particular musical policy. They left it to us and Leslie Paul, the pianist and leader, wrote all the arrangements. There was a vibraphonist, doubling on drums and percussion. That was Peter Shade at first and then various people took over. Johnny Van Derrick played violin and doubled on an exotic Turkish darbuka drum he had brought home from his travels. Leslie wasn't a jazz player but could handle anything as an accompanist and Peter (who also played flute) and especially Johnny were good improvisors so we played jazz pieces like 'Soft Winds' and 'Sweet Georgia Brown'.

I worked with Peter and Johnny away from the hotel too. Johnny sometimes put together a group for radio broadcasts and I did one of those and also played on a record Peter Shade made. They were top players and did a range of things but the Churchill's pay and conditions were so good that the job there took priority.

The staff were well treated on the whole. Each year at the beginning of May we would play dance music for the staff party so most of the employees knew us. At Christmas there was always a hamper to bring home: a turkey and bottles of wine. The staff would line up and file into a room to be given this stuff. Five years after the job began we were each presented with a brass clock and after the tenth anniversary Leslie and Johnny were given a gold watch. But I had started after them and was a few days short of ten years when the hotel closed to be sold, so I missed the watch. It was quite a happy ship, as you would expect of a well-run place, and we were given a full month's holiday each year. People tended to work there for a long time if they did their job efficiently and if they didn't they were out.

The owner of the building that housed the Churchill Hotel would often come to the restaurant, buy us the best champagne and keep us playing after everyone else had left. We were his favourite group. He was very friendly with Harold Wilson, the Prime Minister at the time, and Wilson came to a party at the hotel. In fact there were a number of parties for politicians. Then on March 16th 1976 Wilson suddenly announced to the nation that he planned to resign as Prime Minister and two weeks later a farewell party took place at 10 Downing Street with the Ten Four providing the music. Johnny Van Derrick, who suffered from coronary problems for years, had just had the first of his heart attacks and was in hospital so we had to use another violinist. I lent Wilson my personal microphone for his speech and old Harold was quite amusing. It was a jolly affair with Morecambe and Wise among the guests and Eric Morecambe sang 'On Ilkley Moor' in a duet with Wilson. The next day the *Evening Standard* ran a feature about the party under the headline, 'It's the Harold and Eric Show: Putting on the Style at Farewell to No. 10'.

On weekdays I could do other daytime work such as schools concerts with Michael Garrick or recordings and I always had Sundays free. If something very special came up I'd put in a dep at the hotel, as in September 1977 when I played in a group on stage at the Coliseum in Mark Elder's opera about the Haitian hero Toussaint L'Ouverture.

Earlier that year I started working every Saturday afternoon at Dingwall's in Camden with Iggy Quail on piano and the drummer Laurie Morgan. The three of us already had a regular gig on Sundays at the Stapleton pub in Finsbury Park and that association, first at the Stapleton and then at a series of other congenial north London venues, lasted for 25 years until Iggy died in August 2000. From the beginning, at both the Stapleton and Dingwalls, it was a very free and easy setup and musicians, some semi-pro or amateur, would sit in with us, families with children would come to enjoy the music, and at Dingwalls well-known jazz stars visiting London sometimes dropped in to listen or play.

Iggy and I hit it off straight away. Our backgrounds were

similar in some ways. He had studied classical piano back home in Guyana so we shared West Indian roots and a similar approach. I liked the way he played. He had the same sort of ideas about harmony that I had, he would voice chords in a way I liked and he knew better than anyone how to accompany my bowed/hummed bass solos, always giving strong, two-handed support. He never wanted to push himself into the limelight on the jazz scene and spent much of his career working in small clubs, often with other West Indians. I met him first when we were booked with Johnny Griffin and Jon Hendricks to record music for a short film in the early 1970s. Before that he had worked on the Latin American and Caribbean music circuits around London so our paths hadn't crossed at all.

Not only the music attracted people but also Iggy's personality. He had the loudest voice ever! Wherever he was, his hearty laugh could be heard above everything. He directed proceedings from the piano, chatting as he played and calling to people if he felt like it. As they passed the piano, they would say, 'Hello, Iggy. We'll have a talk in the break.' It was totally relaxed and people felt uninhibited about coming up to play. We made that easy right from the beginning. Of course, people who wanted to play with us had to observe the professional etiquette. If they wanted to solo they had to make sure not to play off-mike because the audience quickly loses interest if they can't hear properly. Also, if someone came on the stand without bothering to tune his instrument properly, Iggy would tell the guy in no uncertain terms to go away and tune up. He wouldn't be allowed back on the stand until that was done. Lack of care in things like that is discourteous to the other musicians. But, while we were tough on people who took advantage or didn't bother enough, we always tried to be encouraging.

I always remembered how grateful I had been, when I started out as a musician, if somebody invited me to play with them. Getting up and playing your best with sympathetic established musicians was the way to become familiar with tunes and different ways of playing. Nowadays there are very few chances for young musicians to do that. So we welcomed guys who wanted to play and we brought in our friends to blow as well. Trumpeters Les Condon and Jim Dvorak, altoist Dudu Pukwana, drummer John Stevens and lots of other musicians came to play. In the break, near the end of the session, local people who fancied themselves as singers would come on stage and sing what they wanted. They'd bring friends to hear them and there would be a real party atmosphere. It wasn't a totally serious musical event and the main thing was that everyone enjoyed themselves with music at the centre of it all. Nothing was planned and it was just a lot of fun. We felt we were part of the community, working in the locality and trying to give something to it, and people who lived in that community could give what they could too and be actively involved in the whole thing. It was just a big party for everyone. That was certainly the idea.

Afterwards we would hang around and talk about music and occasionally there would be other work too: we would sometimes play for private parties or at gatherings at my tennis club and in 1996 we were on the bill for the Crouch End Festival which was very memorable because there was a great atmosphere and, for some reason, the trio's music took off particularly well that day.

I still do Sunday sessions. It's a good way to make music. It draws people in and music is a big enough field for everyone to find some enjoyment in it. On the other hand, the music scene is full of enclaves. For example, Laurie Morgan, who I still play with every week, started out in the Club Eleven days. He is one of the pioneers of modern jazz in Britain. But in those days our paths never crossed and it was only when we began at the Stapleton that I got to know him through Iggy. We were working in different sections of the business. You get to know the musicians you work with.

......

Looking back now I can say that I've certainly enjoyed my musical life. There has been plenty of variety and I've never had time to get bored. Fortunately the contexts have been ones I've usually found satisfying. You have to compromise because you must earn a living but I've not had to compromise in ways I've been unhappy with. It must be purgatory when you always hate the music you have to play. I organised the non-musical side of my life so that I didn't have to be forced into situations where that could happen. I've been blessed with a wonderful home and family and I've worked with a lot of great musicians. Joe Harriott was certainly unlike any of the others. He was a musical genius and now I wish perhaps I could have known him better. But it wasn't possible. Shared West Indian origins weren't enough to overcome everything else that was different in our backgrounds and outlook.

I've been back to Jamaica a couple of times. The first time was after my father died and it felt strange. In was nearly thirty years after I had left for Britain but there were parts of downtown Kingston that I remembered. I went back for the second time in the 1980s to play for the celebrations for the 25th anniversary of Independence (Jamaica became a self-governing member of the old West Indies Federation in 1958 and then fully independent in 1962). I took my bass and stayed for a week. The music was nice and the hotels and the area where I stayed were very pleasant indeed. But that was a contrast with the derelict parts. When I arrived and drove from the airport through Kingston I was horrified how broken down some of it looked. That's sad to see when you know how it used to be. There are parts where the gangs get together now and make a lot of trouble especially at election time.

I can't think of anything I regret in my life. I'm glad I took the career decisions I did. It was risky but I think I did the right things because happiness depends on fulfilment, being able to do things you love doing and to earn money doing them. To have to do something you don't care much about, that you cannot put your heart and soul into, means you are not fulfilled. You have to have faith in yourself and be prepared to face hardships, nurturing your talent to make yourself strong when you face adversity and discrimination. Of course, the jazz world has its familiar problems but I've kept away from the bad, self-destructive sides of the jazz life and tried to prove through my own experience that they aren't essential for the creation of good music.

Music covers an enormous range but the more of it you can participate in the better, so long as it's good and wholesome. Not to be limited in what you can do and to be able to take part in many different ways makes life interesting. That means equipping yourself to be able take on whatever you may want to do and to be always in demand in some context or other. My advice to a young musician now would be practise, practise, practise. You have to develop a good enough technique to be able to play whatever comes in to your head and it takes dedication: hours, days, weeks, years. There is no way to a good technique other than hard work.

The most efficient way to practise is to start with scales and arpeggios. That's vital. And you need to learn all the different positions in which the same set of notes can be played. As you move up the instrument your fingers get closer together. You can't use the same stretch to get the same result from the bottom as you would at the top, so you need to learn the positions and how your hand has to be shaped as you move up the instrument. You have to learn to do that absolutely instinctively.

Playing to records is very useful. When I started I would write down the notes the bassist on the record played and then try to play those notes with the record. That's a very good way of doing it: write the music out and then play it note for note as the bass player is playing it. It takes a lot of work but it's worthwhile if you hear something good like the duets with Ellington and Jimmy Blanton. I wrote out Blanton's lines and practised them for weeks.

You need to practise first with the bow to hear the pitch of the notes correctly, to get them absolutely accurate and stay in tune. It's very important to have the instrument perfectly in tune, which is possible only if you tune with harmonics and that needs to be done using the bow. Another obvious piece of advice is to get the very best instrument you can. A good instrument is expensive but always get the best you can.

My old bass still sits over on its stand in the corner. Of course, I'd never part with it. I have two others but this is my favourite. It's the instrument on which I accompanied Johnny Claes, the Caribbean Trio, Reinhardt and Grappelli, Ray Ellington, Tito Burns, Harriott, Garrick and all the rest. It somehow embodies all those musical memories and it's part of the continuity of my life in jazz. I've owned it through my whole career and it has shared almost all my adventures in music. Now, as I look back, I'm sure I wouldn't have wanted to miss any of those experiences. Music has been good to me since I yearned all those years ago as a young boy back in Jamaica to become a musician. It has paid me back handsomely for the effort needed to master the art of playing it. Music still gives me immense pleasure and enriches my existence every day. I'm sure it always will.

Sources

The following list includes all publications cited in the text as well as others that provided information for it or helped to focus questions and jog memories in the recorded conversations on which this book is based (RC).

Books and articles

ANON, 'The Ray Ellington Quartet', *Checkers: A Monthly Journal in Black and White*, Vol. 1, No. 3, November 1948, pp. 14-15.

Arun Das BANDARANAIKE, 'Freedom in Fusion: John Mayer', *Sunday Times* (Sri Lanka), May 16 1999 (http//www.lacnet.org/suntimes/990516/plus2.html. Visited January 5 2000).

Chris BLACKFORD, 'In Search of Joe Harriott', in Blackford ed, *Joe Harriott*, pp. 17-27.

— ed, *Joe Harriott: Forgotten Father of European Free Jazz*. Special issue, *Rubberneck* no. 25. Basingstoke, 1997.

Brian BLAIN, 'I Remember Phil', in Cotterrell ed, *Jazz Now*, pp. 25-38.

Don BOHNING, 'Sir Philip Sherlock, 98, historian', *Miami Herald*, December 6 2000 (http://www.rose-hulman.edu/-delacova/culture/sherlock.htm. Visited September 20 2002).

Ian CARR, *Music Outside: Contemporary Jazz in Britain*. London: Latimer, 1973.

John CHILTON, *Who's Who of British Jazz*. London: Cassell, 1997.

Jack COOKE, Review of Harriott/Mayer *Indo-Jazz Fusions II* LP, *Jazz Monthly*, June 1968 (includes a reference to hearing Harriott and Dizzy Reece rehearsing free form at the Marquee in 1958).

—, 'Transcending the Ordinary: Memories of Joe Harriott', in Blackford ed, *Joe Harriott*, pp. 28-29.

Roger COTTERRELL, 'A Joe Harriott Memorial', in Cotterrell and Tepperman, *Joe Harriott Memorial*, reprinted in Blackford ed, *Joe Harriott*, pp. 4-12.

—, 'Joe Harriott', *The Wire*, No. 4, Summer 1983, pp. 15-16.

— ed, *Jazz Now: The Jazz Centre Society Guide*. London: Quartet, 1976.

— and Barry TEPPERMAN, *Joe Harriott Memorial: A Bio-Discography*. Ilford: private publication, 1974.

Iain CRUICKSHANK, 'Coleridge Goode', *Jazz Journal*, August 1987, pp. 10-11.

Bob DAWBARN, 'The Next Step?', *Melody Maker*, September 10 1960, p. 12 (the quotes from Joe Harriott and Pat Smythe on pp.

144-5 are from this source).

Charles DELAUNAY, *Django Reinhardt*, translated by Michael James. London: Jazz Book Club/Cassell, 1963.

John FORDHAM, *Jazz Man: The Amazing Story of Ronnie Scott and His Club*. London: Kyle Cathie, 1986.

—, 'Visionary Who Had All the Vibes' (Kenny Graham), *The Guardian*, March 3 1997.

Charles FOX, Notes to Christopher Logue/ Tony Kinsey Quintet *Red Bird* EP (Parlophone GEP 8765), 1959.

—, Review of Michael Garrick *October Woman* LP, *Jazz Monthly*, August 1965.

Mark GARDNER, Review of Michael Garrick *October Woman* LP, *Jazz Journal*, June 1965.

Jim GODBOLT, *A History of Jazz in Britain* (2 volumes). London: Quartet, 1984 and 1989.

Kitty GRIME, *Jazz at Ronnie Scotts*. London: Robert Hale, 1979.

Max HARRISON, 'David Mack and Serial Jazz', *Jazz Monthly*, October 1965, pp. 12-17.

Tony HARRISON, 'Julie Dawn: Danceband singer who found new fame as radio's sympathetic ear', *The Guardian*, May 29 2000.

Phyllis HARTNOLL and Peter FOUND eds, *Concise Oxford Companion to the Theatre*. Oxford: Oxford University Press, 1992.

Joe HARRIOTT, Notes to *Free Form* LP (see below).

—, Notes to *Abstract* LP (see below), reprinted as 'The Truth About Free Form Jazz' in Blackford ed, *Joe Harriott*, pp. 30-31.

Dilip HIRO, *Black British, White British: A History of Race Relations in Britain*. London: Grafton, 1991.

Jorgen Grunnet JEPSEN, *Jazz Records* (11 volumes). Holte, Denmark: Karl Erik Knudsen, 1963-70.

Max JONES, 'This Is Our Big Chance', *Melody Maker*, August 19 1961, p. 7 (the quote from Joe Harriott on p. 150 is from this source).

—, 'Joe Harriott: Ten Years After', *Melody Maker*, July 6 1971, p. 32 (the quote from Joe Harriott on p. 179 is from this source).

Barry KERNFELD ed, *New Grove Dictionary of Jazz*. London: Macmillan, 1988.

Jeff KRUGER, Notes to *Jazz at the Flamingo* CD (Ember FBB 911), 1995.

Colin LARKIN ed, *The Virgin Encyclopedia of Jazz*. London: Virgin Books, 1999.

Ethel MARSON, *George Davis Goode: The Man and His Work*. Kingston, Jamaica: private publication, 1964 (the quote from the *Jamaica Times* on p. 7 is from this source).

Terry E. MARTIN, 'Joe Harriott', *Jazz Monthly*, January 1965, reprinted in Blackford ed, *Joe Harriott*, pp. 13-16.

Jack MASSARIK, 'Coleridge Goode', *The Wire* No. 4, 1983, pp. 17-19.

Tony MIDDLETON, Carl Barriteau', *Jazz Journal*, October 1998, p. 19.

—, *Joe Harriott Bio/discography*. London: TM Publications, 1996.

—, *Johnny Claes: A Bio/Discography*. London: TM Publications, 1994.

Alun MORGAN, 'Alan Clare', *Jazz Journal*, February 1994, p. 22.

—, 'Carlo Kramer Esquire', *Jazz Journal*, June 1976, pp. 8-9.

Philip NANTON, 'Shake Keane's Poetic Legacy', in Sandra Courtman ed, *Society For Caribbean Studies Annual Conference Papers*, vol 1, 2000 (http://www.scsonline.freeserve.co.uk/olvol1. html. Visited January 10 2001).

Stuart NICHOLSON, *Ella Fitzgerald* [1993]. London: Orion reprint, 2001.

Harvey PEKAR, Review of Joe Harriott Quintet *Abstract* LP, *Down Beat*, November 21 1963.

Brian PRIESTLEY, 'Pat Smythe: A Sad Loss', *The Wire* No. 4, 1983, p. 17.

David REYNOLDS, *Rich Relations: The American Occupation of Britain 1942-1945*. London: Phoenix, 2000.

Jeremy ROBSON, Notes to Jeremy Robson / Michael Garrick Quintet, *Blues for the Lonely* EP (Columbia SEG 8244), 1963.

Michael SHERA, Review of Joe Harriott Quintet *High Spirits* LP, *Jazz Journal*, March 1965.

Geoffrey SMITH, *Stéphane Grappelli: A Biography*. London: Pavilion Books / Michael Joseph, 1987 (details of the Grappelli film on pp. 68-9 are from this source).

John STEVENSON, *British Society 1914-45*. Harmondsworth: Penguin, 1984.

Polly THOMAS and Adam VAITILINGAM, *The Rough Guide to Jamaica* 2nd edn. London: Rough Guide, 2000.

Val WILMER, 'The Anger Behind a Free Form of Jazz' (Shake Keane), *The Guardian*, November 13 1997 (the quote on p. 141 is from this source).

—, 'Coleridge Goode: The Master of the Bass', *Flamingo* Vol. 3 No. 8, May 1964.

—, 'The Dukes of Suave' (Ray Ellington Quartet), *Mojo*, May 2001, pp. 22-23.

—, 'Harlem Nights in Deepest Mayfair' (Lauderic Caton), *The Guardian*, February 19 1999 (the quote on p. 45 is from this source).

—, 'Joe Harriott: Jazz Abstractionist', *Down Beat*, September 10 1964.

—, 'London Jazzman Who Cared Nothing for Fame and Fortune as Long as He Could Play His Piano' (Iggy Quail), *The Guardian*, September 4 2000.

—, *Mama Said There'd Be Days Like This: My Life in the Jazz World*. London: Women's Press, 1989 (the quote on p. 131 is from this source).

—, 'Melodic Master of Guitar' (Laurie Deniz), *The Guardian*, March 28 1996.

John WICKES, *Innovations in British Jazz 1960-1980*. Chelmsford: Soundworld, 1999.

Cecil Blazer WILLIAMS, 'Ellsworth McGranahan 'Shake' Keane', *The News* (Kingstown, St. Vincent and the Grenadines), November 14 1997.

Records

All recorded in London. Coleridge Goode plays on all records other than those indicated by [*].

Tito Burns Sextet, 'Festival Hall', 'A Lesson in Bop', etc. (recorded 1951) reissued on *Soho Bop: Modern Jazz from Soho's Legendary Esquire Label* Coolnote CD 30373 00067 (CD).

Caribbean Trio + Bertie King (from 'Jazz Matinée' BBC Radio broadcast August 1947, introduced by Jack Jackson) and Alan Clare Trio (recordings from Studio Club, 1950s). Privately produced CD, Coleridge Goode collection.

Ray Ellington Quartet, *The Three Bears* (recordings 1948-9) reissued 2000 on Avid AMSC 697 (CD).

Michael Garrick Quintet, *October Woman*, Argo ZDA 33 (LP) (recorded 1964).

Michael Garrick, *Anthem*, Argo EAF/ZFA29 (EP) (recorded 1965).

Michael Garrick Sextet, *Promises*, Argo ZDA 36 (LP) (recorded 1965).

Michael Garrick Quintet with John Smith (reader), 'Jazz for Five', on Garrick's *Black Marigolds*, Argo (S)DA 88 (LP) (recorded 1966 [*]).

Michael Garrick, *Jazz Praises At St. Paul's*, Airborne NBP 0021 (LP) (recorded 1968).

Michael Garrick, *Mr. Smith's Apocalypse*, Argo ZAGF 1 (LP) (recorded 1971).

Michael Garrick Orchestra, 'Swallows on the Water', on Garrick's *For Love of Duke... and Ronnie*, Jazz Academy JAZA 4 (CD) (recorded 1995-6 [*]).

Stéphane Grappelli and his Quintet (including George Shearing, Coleridge Goode, Ray Ellington), 'Yellow House Stomp', 'Red-O-Ray', 'Channel Crossing' and 'In the Mood' (recorded 1947). First two titles issued as Decca F8917 (78rpm).

Joe Harriott Quintet, *Blue Harriott*, Columbia SEG 7939 (EP) (recorded 1959).

Joe Harriott Quintet, BBC 'Jazz Club' broadcast, August 13 1959. Private recording, Coleridge Goode collection.

Joe Harriott Quintet, *Southern Horizons*, Columbia SEG 8070 (EP) (recorded 1960. The recordings on this EP together with those on *Blue Harriott* were also released together in the US as *Southern Horizons*, Jazzland JLP 937S LP).

Joe Harriott Quintet with Frank Holder, BBC 'Jazz Club' broadcast, Bath Festival, May 26 1960. Private recording, Coleridge Goode collection.

Joe Harriott Quintet, *Free Form*, Jazzland JLP 949S (LP) (recorded 1960), reissued 1998 on Redial 538-184-2 (CD).

Joe Harriott Quintet, *Abstract*, Columbia 33SX 1477 / Capitol 10351 (LP) (recorded 1961-2), reissued 1998 on Redial 538-183-2 (CD).

Joe Harriott Quintet, *Movement*, Columbia 33SX 1627 (LP) (recorded 1963).

Joe Harriott Quintet, *High Spirits*, Columbia 33SX 1692 (LP) (recorded 1964).

Joe Harriott, *Genius*, Jazz Academy JAZA 6 (CD) (live recordings, issued 2000, of the Joe Harriott Quintet 1961, Michael Garrick 1960s groups, etc.).

Joe Harriott Quintet, *Swings High*, Melodisc SLP 12-150 (LP) (recorded 1967).

Joe Harriott - John Mayer Double Quintet, *Indo-Jazz Suite*, Columbia SX 6025/ Atlantic SD1465 (LP) (recorded 1966), reissued 1999 on Koch Jazz KOC CD8512 (CD).

Joe Harriott - John Mayer Double Quintet, *Indo-Jazz Fusions*, Columbia SX 6122/ Atlantic SD1482 (LP) (recorded 1967), reissued 1998 on Redial 538-048-2 (CD).

Joe Harriott - John Mayer Double Quintet, *Indo-Jazz Fusions II*, Columbia SX 6215 (LP) (recorded 1968), reissued 1998 on Redial 538-048-2 (CD).

Leslie 'Jiver' Hutchinson Orchestra, 'Swing Low, Sweet Chariot' and 'Big Top Boogie' (recorded 1944), issued 2001 on *Black British Swing* (by various artists), Topic TSCD 781 (CD).

Shake Keane Quintet, *In My Condition*, Columbia SEG 8140 (EP) (recorded 1961).

Shake Keane and the Boss Men (sextet), *Bossa Negra*, Columbia SEG 8239 (EP) (recorded 1962).

Shake Keane / Michael Garrick Quartet, *A Case of Jazz*, Airborne NBP 0002 (EP) (recorded 1963).

Shake Keane (sextet), *That's the Noise*, Ace of Clubs ACL 1219 (LP) (recorded 1960s).

David Mack, *New Directions*, Columbia 33SX 1670 (LP) (recorded 1964).

Django Reinhardt and the Quintet of the Hot Club of France, 'Coquette', 'Django's Tiger', 'Embraceable You', 'Echoes of France', 'Love's Melody', 'Belleville', 'Nuages' and 'Liza' (recorded 1946), reissued on *Django Reinhardt 1944-1946*, Classics 945 (CD).

Jeremy Robson with the Michael Garrick Quintet, *Blues for the Lonely*, Argo EAF 115 (EP) (recorded 1965).

Ten Four, 'Gershwin Medley', 'Für Elise', 'Sometimes When We Touch', 'Soft Winds', 'I Concentrate on You', 'Send In the Clowns', 'Pavanne' and 'Sweet Georgia Brown' (recorded c.1981), on *Music at the Churchill* (by various artists), Loews 1 (LP).

Ken Vandermark's Joe Harriott Project, *Straight Lines*, Atavistic ALP115 (CD) (recorded 1998 [*])

Other sources

'Jazz Legends: Joe Harriott' (radio broadcast). Julian Joseph in conversation with Michael Garrick. Including excerpts from a 1963 interview with Joe Harriott. BBC Radio 3, Friday 22 March 2002 (the quotes from Harriott on p. 158 are from this source).

'The Jazz Islands: Joe Harriott' (radio broadcast), presented by Ben Watson, including recorded contributions from Val Wilmer, Coleridge Goode, Frank Holder and Joe Harriott. BBC Radio 3, February 12 2000 (the quote from Frank Holder on p. 160 is from this source).

'Ray Ellington: A Talk by Val Wilmer', Durning Library, Kennington, London, October 14 2000 (the material on Ellington's early life is from this source and used with Val Wilmer's kind permission).

Alpha School: http://www.bbc.co.uk/radio2/reggae_soul/island_rock/artists/sisterignatius.shtml (visited September 10 2002)

Goon Show: http://www.thegoonshow.co.uk/goonography/series1.html and http://www.goonshow.org.uk/goonistry.htm (visited December 8 2001).

Jamaica: http://www.discoverjamaica.com/history6.htm (visited May 23 2002).

Queen Mary: http://www.queenmary.com/QMweb/html/hist.html (visited September 10 2002).

Billy Thorburn: http://www.users.tsn.cc/kvxg/bthorht.htm and http://www.jabw.demon.co.uk/thorburn.htm (visited August 8 2002).

Arthur Wint: http://caribbean.halloffame.tripod.com/Arthur_Wint.html (visited September 20 2002).

Personal acknowledgements

Warm thanks to Michael Garrick for supplying photos and for details of his musical activities, Eddie and Janet Cook and *Jazz Journal International* for help with photos, Kevin Henriques and Tito Burns for information, and Val Wilmer for providing copies of her *Flamingo* and *Mojo* articles, helpful leads in last-minute checking of a few elusive facts in the manuscript, and an enjoyable afternoon's conversation about contributions of black musicians to jazz in Britain and the USA. Above all, thanks to Ann Cotterrell for being the best of editors and for support in all aspects of this project.

Index

Other jazz books from Northway

*Gold, Doubloons
and Pieces of Eight
by
Harry Gold*

The autobiography of
saxophonist and band
leader Harry Gold – a
wonderful memoir of
the early years of jazz
in Britain

*207 pages plus 39 gloss
photos.*

£10.99
ISBN 0 9537040 0 9   2000

*Notes from
a Jazz Life
by
Digby Fairweather*

*Jazz cornetist, band
leader and broadcaster
Digby Fairweather tells
of his life and career
with candid, warm and
hilarious anecdotes.*

*Illustrations by Peter
Manders and Humphrey
Lyttelton. 183 pages.*

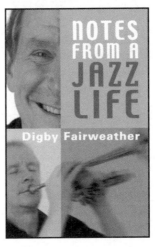

£7.99
ISBN 0 9537040 1 7   2002

Northway 39 Tytherton Road London N19 4PZ Info@northwaybooks.com

Coleridge Goode's career has long been at the heart of the jazz world. Known as a 'prince' among bassists, he has recorded with Django Reinhardt, Stéphane Grappelli, Ray Nance, George Shearing and countless other jazz stars. Here, assisted by jazz writer Roger Cotterrell, he recalls his life and career including his Jamaica childhood and arrival in Britain in the 1930s, the lively wartime London club scene, the Ray Ellington Quartet of Goon Show fame and his long association with altoist Joe Harriott, the brilliant but tragic pioneer of European free jazz. Always among the innovators, he has helped blend jazz with Indian music, serial compositions, choral works and poetry and he tells candidly about the challenges and rewards of the jazz life as well as the destructive aspects he has seen – especially racial discrimination and drugs. A contributor to many of the most exciting jazz developments of the past half century, Coleridge Goode is a thoughtful witness to a fascinating part of jazz history.

ISBN 0-9537040-2-5

9 780953 704026 >

northway
publications

£9.99